In Valiant Company

Ben O'Dowd was born in Perth in 1918 as Bernard Shelley O'Dowd. He had little education, leaving school at the age of fourteen during the Great Depression. When World War II broke out in 1939, he was employed underground on a mine in the Western Australian goldfields. He enlisted in the Second AIF immediately, and was allocated to 2/11th Australian Infantry Battalion. He served in the Middle East and was wounded in the Libyan campaign. With the entry of Japan into the war, the battalion returned to Australia and saw service in New Guinea. At Wewak in June 1945, while acting as a platoon commander, he was awarded a field commission. At the end of the war O'Dowd went to Japan with the Occupation Force, where he was offered a Regular Army commission.

When the Korean War broke out, the 3rd Battalion of the Royal Australian Regiment was committed as part of the British Commonwealth Brigade. Initially O'Dowd was the HQ Company Commander, but in November 1950 took command of A Company, the "Valiant Company" chronicled in this book. From Korea he went on to serve for two years with the British Army on anti-terrorist operations during the Malayan Emergency. He then held several staff appointments prior to leaving the Army in 1973, after thirty-four years of unbroken service.

IN VALIANT COMPANY

BEN O'DOWD

The University of Queensland

First published 2000 by University of Queensland Press
Box 42, St Lucia, Queensland 4067 Australia

© Bernard (Ben) O'Dowd 2000

This book is copyright. Except for private study, research,
criticism or review, as permitted under the Copyright Act,
no part of this book may be reproduced, stored in a retrieval
system, or transmitted in any form or by any means without
prior written permission. Enquiries should be made to the
publisher.

Typeset by University of Queensland Press
Printed in Australia by McPherson's Printing Group

Distributed in the USA and Canada by
International Specialized Book Services, Inc.,
5804 N.E. Hassalo Street, Portland, Oregon 97213–3640

ISBN 0 7022 3146 0

The photo of the author on p. i was taken just after the
Korean War.

CONTENTS

List of maps   vii
Abbreviations   viii
Foreword: by Jack Gallaway   xi
Preface   xiii

1. To Korea   *1*
2. The Battle of Pakchon   *17*
3. Assembling the Team   *30*
4. The Running-in Phase   *38*
5. Running Away   *47*
6. The Bridge at Yopa-ri   *52*
7. The Slow Road from Hayu-ri to Uijongbu   *58*
8. Activities at Uijongbu   *64*
9. Tokchong: A Perilous Withdrawal   *75*
10. On the Run Again   *81*
11. Thirty-two Kilometres of No Man's Land   *86*
12. Patrol to Ichon   *94*
13. Patrol to Chipyong-ni   *105*
14. Attack on Hill 195, "Doctor"   *112*
15. Attack on Hill 410, "Woodbine"   *120*
16. The God Botherers   *129*
17. Attack on Chisan   *133*
18. About Hospitalisation   *138*

19. Attack on "Sardine"   *143*
20. Plan Audacious   *150*
21. The Battle of Kapyong   *154*
Epilogue   *187*

Appendix A: Overture to Battle   *196*
Appendix B: Rifle Company Casualties, September 1950
           to April 1951   *200*
Notes   *203*
Index   *209*

LIST OF MAPS

1. Korea: overview of 3 RAR operations, 28 September 1950–24 April 1951
2. Battle of Pakchon, 5–6 November 1950
3. 3 RAR movements, 2–5 December 1950
4. Company positions at Yopa-ri bridge
5. Withdrawal from Tokchong, 1 January 1951
6. 3 RAR movements, 1–4 January 1951
7. Withdrawal to Changhowon-ni
8. Patrol to Ichon
9. Enemy attacks at Ichon
10. 3 RAR movements, 14–15 February 1951. Attack on "Doctor"
11. "Doctor" battlefield
12. 3 RAR movements 12 February–11 March 1951, including "Woodbine" and Chisan.
13. 3 RAR movements, 1–16 April 1951, to reach "Sardine" and "Salmon"
14. The Kansas Line, 22 April 1951
15. Proposed plan "Audacious"
16. Proposed blocking positions of 27 British Commonwealth Brigade, 23 April 1951
17. Actual blocking positions occupied by 27 BCB, 23–24 April 1951
18. Layout of A Company positions, 1900 hrs, 23–24 April 1951
19. Layout of D Company positions, 23–24 April 1951
20. 27 BCB situation, 24 April 1951, including the withdrawal route

ABBREVIATIONS

AATTV	Australian Army Training Team Vietnam.
1 A&SH	1st Battalion, Argyll and Sutherland Highlanders
2iC	Second in Command
2 PPCLI	2nd Battalion, Princess Patricia's Canadian Light Infantry
3 RAR	3rd Battalion, Royal Australian Regiment
AB	Airborne
ACT	Air Contact Team
B Ech	Administrative personnel, stores and vehicles
Brig	Brigadier
Bug out	Hasty and undisciplined retreat (American)
Capt	Captain
CCF	Communist Chinese Forces
CO	Commanding Officer
Cpl	Corporal
CSM	Company Sergeant Major
FDL	Forward Defence Line
FEch	Fighting Echelon (vehicles and personnel)
FOO	Forward Observation Officer (Artillery)
Gen	General
GMC	Six-wheel drive US vehicle used for general transport
GOC	General Officer Commanding
KSLI	King's Shropshire Light Infantry
KOSB	King's Own Scottish Borderers
LAC	Leading Aircraftsman
Lt	Lieutenant
Lt Col	Lieutenant Colonel
Maj	Major
MFC	Mobile Fire Controller
MLR	Main Line of Resistance (US term)

ABBREVIATIONS

MMG	Medium Machine Gun
1MX	1st Battalion, Middlesex Regiment
NK	North Korea
OC	Officer Commanding
O Group	Orders Group (CO, commanders and others who were assembled to receive orders for operations)
Inf	Infantry
RAP	Regimental Aid Post
RCT	Regimental Combat Team
Rear Link	Communications between brigade and battalion HQs
R & R	Rest and Recuperation
RMO	Regiment Medical Officer
RNZA	Royal New Zealand Artillery
ROK	Republic of Korea
RSM	Regimental Sergeant Major
Sgt	Sergeant
Tac HQ	Tactical Headquarters (a small operational headquarters)
WOI	Warrant Officer First Class
WOII	Warrant Officer Second Class

FOREWORD

On 23 April 1951, the 3rd Battalion was attacked by elements of a Chinese Communist Field Army numbering some 7000 men. This force was desperate to break through in the Kapyong Valley in order to outflank the capital of South Korea, Seoul, and cut off more than half of the United Nations Army. Only the understrength British Commonwealth Brigade stood in their path, and in the vanguard stood 3 RAR supported by a regiment of New Zealand Artillery. For most of that night, and all the next day, this battalion's four rifle companies — less than 400 men — were all that stood between the CCF and victory in the Korean War. By sundown on Anzac Day, the Chinese had ceased their offensive and commenced withdrawing. It was a victory worthy of the Anzac tradition.

Major O'Dowd commanded A Company at Kapyong, a posting that he had held since mid-November 1950. At Kapyong it was A Company who "drew the crow", an experience to which its Diggers had become accustomed. How and why this happened, and the result of this epic encounter, marks the climax of O'Dowd's story

Kapyong was the last of eleven engagements in which A Company took part in the first eight months of the Korean War, engagements which cost the company 163 casualties, almost twice its posted strength. Kapyong was by far the bloodiest of these, but A Company's strength and morale were as steadfast as ever. It was a battle fought at night in desperate circumstances. Despite the loss of half their strength killed and wounded, O'Dowd's men fought gallantly, coolly, skilfully. They simply refused to be beaten. They left the battlefield victorious with heads held high, with honour bright.

Grandson and namesake of the famous radical poet, Bernard (Ben) O'Dowd inherited the right genes. He tells a soldier's story, he tells it well and it is most aptly titled. His was a valiant company indeed. He tells of war most bloody in a climate almost as far removed from the Australian environment as is the Arctic; of battles fought against odds of four and five to one; of fire and movement and company attacks "up the guts" in towering mountains against a brave and skilful enemy dug in. He writes of soldiers fighting in desperate defence from shallow scrapes hastily dug in rocky soil, of their man to man battles, hand to hand, and of patrols at night in knee-deep snow and violent bloody ambush with the business being done at arm's length.

Kapyong is the Royal Australian Regiment's primary Battle Honour, and O'Dowd's first-hand description of the battle is unique. *In Valiant Company* tells the whole A Company story and tells it without frills. There are no eulogies, there is no bravado, just the facts. O'Dowd's presentation is both honest and self-effacing. If his story has a hero, it is the Australian Digger. And more specifically, all of those non-pariel Diggers who stood shoulder to shoulder at Kapyong and who emerged victorious from a dozen other engagements, both great and small — the men who made up Major Ben O'Dowd's valiant company. They were no saints, and his honest description of their misdeeds makes this plain, but, saints or sinners, they were O'Dowd's men and his pride in them shines through on every page of the text.

O'Dowd's story is military history at its best, but it is also a rattling good yarn which carries an unchallengeable stamp of authenticity. For any old soldier not to own a copy would be a worse crime than dropping his rifle on parade.

Jack Gallaway

PREFACE

Over the years I have written up the actions fought in Korea by A Company, 3rd Battalion, the Royal Australian Regiment. Most of these have been published in the Royal Australian Regiment Association's journal, *Duty First*, with a view to testing the veracity of my statements against the memories of other Korean veterans. A few years ago the editor of the journal, Peter Cook, suggested that I should arrange these articles in chronological order, fill in the gaps and construct a continuous narrative. *In Valiant Company* is the result.

This narrative projects an intimate view of the fighting men of A Company, and the conditions under which they operated. It also includes some personal memories and reflections.

I am indebted to my son-in-law, Peter Andrewatha, to whom I provided an early draft. Although an interested reader of military subjects he has had no connection with the army, so was able to study the manuscript from the outside. Peter put his finger on areas where I may have confused a non-service reader.

Olwyn Green, the widow of Lt Col Charles Green and an author in her own right, asked to see the manuscript which she returned with numerous helpful comments. Many thanks, Olwyn.

Jack Gallaway, author of *The Last Call of the Bugle*, heard what I was up to and encouraged, cajoled and badgered, keeping me at the project. Whenever I faltered on the job he kick-started me again. I thank Gallaway for both his persistence and assistance.

Finally, I must thank those many A Company veterans who helped to fill in gaps with important details, and for the photographs they so readily provided.

Ben O'Dowd

In Pusan there is hallowed ground,
  A simple cross to mark each mound.
They brought us there from whence we died
  To lie together side by side.

Strange country and a stranger war,
  It made no odds — we knew the score.
We were blood brothers, truth to tell,
  In valiant company when we fell.

      Jack Gallaway, "Last Call of the Bugle"

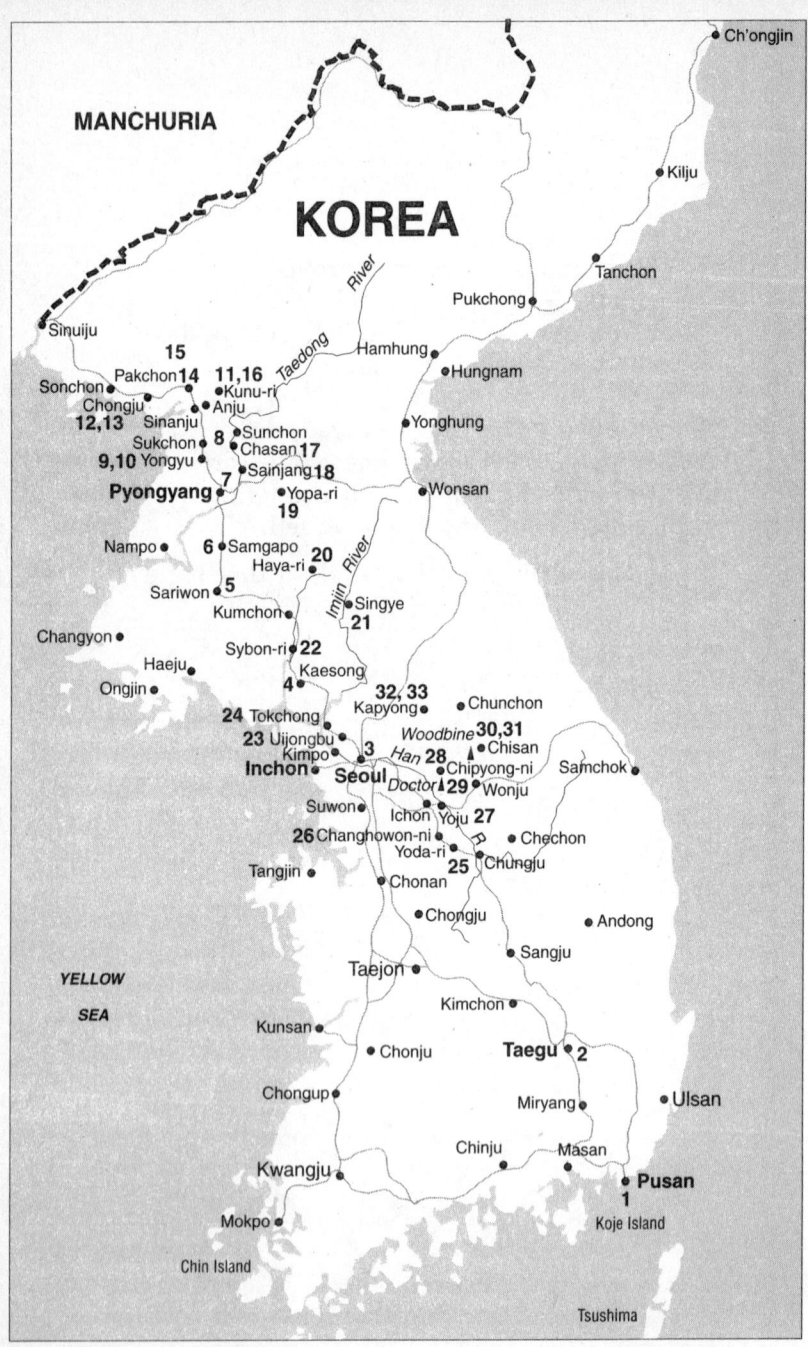

Map 1: Korea: 3 RAR operations, 28 September 1950–24 April 1951

Key

1 28 September: Arrive Pusan. Move by rail to Taegu.
2 30 September: Visit by Brig Coad. Plum Pudding Hills operations.
3 5 October: Air move to Kimpo Airport, Seoul.
4 12 October: 27 BCB joins 1 Cavalry Division at Kaesong. Begins pursuit operations.
5 13 October: 3 RAR lead to Sariwon. Confusion of mingling, enemy and own troops.
6 18 October: A Coy clearing action at Samgapo.
7 20 October: 27 BCB at outskirts of Pyongyang.
8 20 October: US 187 Airborne dropped at Sukchon and Sunchon.
9 21 October: 1 A&SH clears roads towards 187 Airborne at Yongju.
10 22 October: 3 RAR fights Apple Orchard.
11 25 October: Broken Bridge battle.
12 29 October: Battle of Chongju.
13 30 October: Lt Col Green wounded. Died 1 November 1950.
14 5 November: Battle of Pakchon.
15 6–27 November: Minor ops north of Pakchon.
16 27 November: 27 BCB withdraws to Kunu-ri and harbour in river bed.
17 28 November: Withdrawal to Chasan, 3 km south of Sunchon.
Stores dumped to provide troop-carrying vehicles.
18 1 December 0900 hrs: Withdrawal to Sainjang 4.5 km south of Chasan.
1300 hrs: Ordered back to Chasan.
19 2 December: Withdrawal to Yopa-ri. Occupy bridgehead.
20 4 December: Move to Haya-ri. Dispatched to clear US Army ambush next day.
21 6 December: Withdrawal to Singye.
22 8 December: Withdrawal to Sibyon-ni.
23 11 December: Withdrawal to Uijongbu.
18 December: A Coy patrol 112 km to Hyon-ni.
21 December: Recce of South Mountain. Blocking position in event of withdrawal.
24 1 January 1000 hrs: Blocking position at Tokchong. 1500 hrs: Withdrawal from Tokchong.
25 4 January: Withdrawal to Yoda-ri.
26 6 January: Occupy Line D, Changhowon-ni area.
12 January: Patrols to Ichon commence.
20–21 January: A Coy patrol to Ichon.
24 January: UN Forces go over to attack. Contact patrols to US units begin with Mulry, 3 Pl.
25 January: Contact patrols, Jim Young, 6 Pl.
26 January: Contact patrols, Morrison, 7 Pl.
27 January: Contact patrols, Montgomerie, 4 Pl.
28 January: Contact patrols, Beacroft, A Tk Pl.
29 January: Contact patrols, Colin Townsend, 8 Pl.
27 5 February: Move to Yoju.
10 February: Patrols to Chipyong-ni begin.
13 February: A Coy conducts the last patrol to Chipyong-ni.
28 14 February: Chipyong-ni besieged. Move to Chaum-ni valley.
15 February: Hill 195, "Doctor" attack.
17 February: Enemy withdrawal.
29 16 February: Second attack on "Doctor".
30 7 March: Attack on "Woodbine".
31 11 March: Attack on Chisan.
32 1–14 April: Operation "Rugged".
15–16 April: Attacks on "Sardine" and "Salmon".
33 23–24 April: Battle of Kapyong.

ONE

TO KOREA

From the time of its arrival in Korea in September 1950 until the Battle of Kapyong in April 1951, A Company of the 3rd Battalion of the Royal Australian Regiment fought seven major actions. In this time fifty-one fine men of this company were killed, one hundred and fourteen were wounded and five were taken prisoner of war. I took command of this company on 6 November 1950 and commanded it throughout the period described in this book.

From 1949 Australia had been steadily reducing its contribution to the Japanese Occupation Force. By early 1950 the 1st and 2nd Battalions of the Royal Australian Regiment (RAR) had been withdrawn to Australia, with 3rd Battalion scheduled to join them during 1950. Anticipating its withdrawal, 3 RAR had not been reinforced, and by mid-1950 attrition had reduced the unit to three under-strength rifle companies, no Support Company and a skeleton Headquarters Company.

On 25 June 1950 the Republic of North Korea attacked the Republic of South Korea (ROK) across the 38th parallel, the border between the two countries. It rapidly captured the capital of South Korea, Seoul, and continued to drive the ROK army south, down the peninsula. The US 24th Division was committed to the fray but could not halt the enemy advance. The North Korean Army (NKA) continued a relentless pursuit until it had the ROK and US Army forces locked into a tight perimeter around the southern port of Pusan (known as the Pusan Box). In Japan at this time you could get some fairly good odds about the chance of the UN Forces being kicked into the sea.

A desperate call went out from the United Nations for member countries to contribute forces. On 29 June Australia responded by placing RAN ships at the disposal of Commander in Chief, United Nations Forces, General Douglas MacArthur, and on 30 June, 77 Fighter Squadron, RAAF. The first to offer ground troops was Britain with the 28th Brigade, which was being assembled and trained in the UK for Korean service. However, their availability was some months away, so the 27th Brigade, then on garrison duties in Hong Kong, was committed as a stop-gap measure. This brigade consisted of two under-strength battalions — 1st Battalion, the Middlesex Regiment (1 MX), and 1st Battalion, the Argyll and Sutherland Highlanders (1 A&SH) — and no artillery. The 27th Brigade arrived in Korea on 27 August 1950 and was immediately committed to the perimeter of the Pusan Box.

On 26 July 1950 a jubilant air spread throughout the 3rd Battalion when the acting Prime Minister, Arthur Fadden, announced that Australian ground forces would be provided for Korea. 3 RAR was the logical choice for this task, being already in theatre.

The battalion was grossly under strength. To bring it to War Establishment in weapons, vehicles and equipment the necessary items had to be flown and shipped from Australia. Personnel were provided by gutting the other two battalions of the brigade, but this still left a shortfall of some hundreds of men. Recruits were needed not only to bring 3 RAR to War Establishment but also to create a trained reserve to replace casualties and personnel lost through general attrition. In the critically short time frame it was impossible to enlist and train raw recruits. Fortunately, however, there was a large reservoir of battle-hardened

Diggers from World War II who were still eligible for re-enlistment. World War II veterans responded to the call in their hundreds, bringing with them invaluable experience and the technical skills so urgently required. These were the officers and men of "K Force", representing all the Australian Divisions which had fought in the Middle East and New Guinea, plus some ex-British Army men.

The Commanding Officer of 3 RAR at the time was Lt Col F. S. Walsh, who immediately set about preparing the unit for the Korea commitment. After dinner in the Officers Mess it was the custom to tune in to Radio Australia to catch up on home and world affairs. One evening, the group was shocked to hear the newsreader calmly announce that Lt Col Charles Green DSO would take the battalion to Korea. Stan Walsh was embarrassed and justifiably angry at this casual, unethical treatment. The GOC, Gen Sir Horace C. H. Robertson, was no doubt equally angry at not being informed that a senior officer under his command was to be sacked. It seems that people in high places considered that Walsh lacked the necessary battle command experience for the Korean situation.

Charles Green's appointment to command 3 RAR was great news for me. He had been my Commanding Officer in 2/11th Australian Infantry Battalion during the Aitape–Wewak Campaign in New Guinea. It was he who had me commissioned in the field, at Wewak. He arrived at the battalion on 10 September along with the final batch of reinforcements required to bring the battalion to full strength.

Green must have had some misgivings about the situation into which he had been pitchforked. In June 1950 he was halfway through a twelve-month course at the Army Staff College, Queenscliffe, when he was plucked out and sent to Japan to take a battalion into battle. He had but two weeks in which to stamp his authority on the unit and prepare it for whatever Korea should demand. An odd manning situation existed. Officers and men had been drawn in haste from many sources; the CO did not know his officers, the officers did not know each other and, in the main, the men knew neither. Green had a potential "Tower of Babel" situation.

The situation with the officers was also unusual. Every officer of the rank of captain and above, including Lt Col Green, was World War II AIF commissioned. On the other hand, all the Lieutenants except one were recent, untried Royal Military College graduates. (Although untried at that stage, after being tested in battle they rapidly became old hands, and performed extremely well. Within a few months two of them would be killed in action and two wounded.)

There followed some very busy days, issuing vehicles, weapons and associated equipment, kitting out personnel, crating and packing unit and personal gear for storage, making wills, receiving inoculations and vaccinations, and undertaking a plethora of general administration.

Charlie Green did manage one tactical exercise which was conducted in torrential rain. The cooks got practical experience at not being able to operate in a flooded kitchen and the Diggers got experience at working on an empty stomach. When a Digger is cold, tired and hungry he becomes quite eloquent, and junior officers learn a lot about man management.

In this period I saw another lesson meted out to young officers. One of the companies had had a hard day and a long march back to barracks, arriving tired and sweaty. Their three young platoon commanders were seated in the Mess shortly after, freshly showered, neatly dressed and beer in hand. The beer was only half consumed when their World War II vintage company commander appeared, unwashed and in the battledress he had been wearing all day.

"Were hot showers available for your men? Have their feet been inspected for blisters? Were disinfectant foot baths available? Have they had a satisfactory evening meal?"

Blank faces.

"Well, go and find out!"

They didn't really want that beer anyway.

A week or so prior to movement the CO reposted me from 2iC D Company to Commander, Headquarters Company and Battle 2iC. In the infantry battalion of that day the holder of this great, grand and glorious title had a mixture of duties in the field. Apart from command of all troops located within Battalion Headquarters area, his responsibilities were the siting, layout and security of the headquarters. In the advance or attack, the 2iC proper was located at a rear echelon. The idea was that the Battle 2iC should represent 2iC proper at Orders Groups, to keep track of the CO's intentions should a take-over briefing for battalion 2iC become necessary. In practice this was not always possible.

The 15th of September brought an air of dejection into our camp with the news of Gen Douglas MacArthur's seaborne attack on the port for Seoul, Inchon. This master stroke, deep behind the North Korean Army forces at Pusan, effectively threatened their lines of communication, precipitating a desperate scramble back to the shelter of the 38th parallel, from whence they had come, with the UN Army in hot pursuit. From where we stood it appeared that the party was over and we had missed out on the action. Many member countries of the UN were against pursuit into North Korea for fear of bringing China into the conflict, and the possibility of starting World War III. Nevertheless, preparations for our movement went ahead.

On 21 September the battalion moved into the field training area for demonstrations by the Mortar and Medium Machine Gun platoons followed by exercises. Lt Gen Sir Horace Robertson (Red Robbie) attended the demonstrations on the 22nd and at the conclusion gave the order to return to barracks and prepare for embarkation for Korea. A ship was on the way to transport us to the scene of the action. It had been a long day and we all looked forward to a quick run back in transport, to the comforts of barracks and celebration of the good news. Silly us! Charlie Green was not going to be denied his last chance of some training. The vehicle convoy was on its way when he ordered it to return to base empty. That trek back to camp was the longest twenty miles of my marching experience, arriving at barracks at about midnight. I've no doubt it did us good, but from the muttering coming from the rear, I gathered that the Diggers did not share this view.

Married members of the battalion with us during occupation days in Japan had their families in married quarters at Niji Mura village. There were other soldiers with families too that were not recognised by the authorities. Occupation regulation prohibited fraternisation with Japanese but soldiers took little notice of this, and more than a few contrived liaisons with local Japanese women. Some were just living together as man and wife; others had solemnised the union with Japanese Shinto marriage celebrations. As attitudes changed, most of the Japanese Brides managed to migrate to Australia, to settle down happily as accepted and valued members of the community.

At the docks our band belted out its last melodic offering before the instruments went into storage. The bandsmen were now the stretcher bearers who were to administer to our casualties so devotedly in the coming months. There was a noisy crowd of soldiers, family and other well-wishers on the dock to cheer us on our way, along with some tears. Someone made the mandatory farewell speech which was pretty much ignored.

On the opposite side of the ship a short gap separated us from a parallel dock. Here the unofficial Japanese families and other indigenous well-wishers gathered. Although not demonstrative people by nature, this group of locals cheered us too or shed a tear as appropriate.

Arriving in Korea on 28 September 1950 we disembarked at Pusan to the welcome of US and Korean army bands. Then there was a short rail journey to Taegu to bivouac in a dry river bed, to wait for our unit transport and Medium Machine Gun and Mortar Carriers[1] to unload and join us.

On 30 September we had a visit from our brigade commander, Brig B. A. Coad DSO. The 27 Brigade then officially became the "27th British Commonwealth Brigade" (27 BCB). Coad caught the imagination of the Diggers instantly. Being a large man with a pronounced, ruddy nose, the nicknames of Plonky or Penfolds were respectfully appended. The brigadier advised that our immediate tasks were to hunt down the many enemy stragglers by-passed by the rapid UN Army advance north and to locate and destroy ammunition dumps in the area. This was hardly the kind of confrontation we had so keenly anticipated, but Lt Col Green saw it as a means of providing commanders at all levels with practical "on the job" training at patrolling. To some degree it also tested the unit's administration.

That afternoon we were transported to Songju to get on with the search and destroy operations in the Plum Pudding Hills. (Where that name came from I do not know.) On 3 October we took our first casualties when a Weapon Carrier ran into an unmarked minefield, killing Capt Ken Hummerston and Pte Sketckly.

On 4 October all patrols were aborted and the battalion concentrated on preparing for movement next day by air from Taegu to the Seoul airport of Kimpo. At Taegu we were given a demonstration of US Air Force capacity. In one afternoon the entire brigade, the headquarters and three battalions were airlifted in good old DC4s and not so good old C119 Box Cars. The C119 had a large body capable of loading personnel or a heavy tank. From the rear of the body thin twin booms protruded, to accommodate the elevators and rudder. While the troops were lining up ready to board their allocated Box Car, one came in to land. As it touched the tarmac the twin tails broke loose and were dragged down the runway screeching and spitting sparks. Immediately the aircraft came to rest the occupants leapt out, with legs running before they touched the ground, to avoid the threatened conflagration. It did not catch on fire, but the incident did little for the morale of the troops lined up waiting to board Box Cars.

Our transport and carriers had a torturous trip via overcrowded roads and did not marry up with the main body until five days later, 9 October. Although ROK units had already gone over the border, the main topic of conversation was still whether MacArthur would be given political clearance for UN troops to follow them, and invade North Korea.

On 7 October Col Green had informed us that the 1 Cavalry Division was in the process of taking Kaesong, and that when they had secured it, 27 BCB would come under this division's command. The Division took Kaesong on the 9th, and we immediately motored to join them for the push into North Korea.

In spite of their name the 1st Cavalry Division no longer had horses (or armour for that matter); they were standard foot sloggers like ourselves. No doubt somewhere back in history they rode horses, but were subsequently dismounted and did not get around to changing nomenclature. In the Japanese Occupation days they were Gen MacArthur's palace guards, and we became associated with them from time to time. An American friend of mine once unkindly described this division as, "the only cavalry outfit in the world with more horses' arses than horses' heads".

The move into North Korea got under way on 12 October, with the brigade advancing to Kumchon, the Middlesex leading and 3 RAR second in the line of march. Movement was slow and uneventful. On the 13th we took the lead with a platoon of Sherman tanks under command and a company of US 105 mm field artillery.

The idea in pursuit operations is to keep right up with the retreating enemy so he is not encouraged to turn and go in defence. The tactic was to drive in convoy with all possible speed, consistent with general safety. When enemy delaying troops were encountered, the leading company dismounted, mounted a quick attack, and the pursuit continued.

At Sariwon it came about that we pursued faster than the enemy could retreat. Here confused and intermittent fighting commenced due to 24 US Division driving from the south, 7 Cavalry Regiment pushing from the north and 27 BCB driving from the east. In the middle of all this were elements of an NKA Division, and by 1800 hours 27 BCB was in there with them. In the failing light the North Koreans mistook the Australians and the Argylls for Russians, greeting them as saviours with "Ruski, Ruski!" In some cases BCB and enemy vehicles were parked alongside each other. Eventually shots were exchanged and most of the enemy troops surrendered.

An enemy truck was captured by Lt Eric Larson's 6 Platoon.[2] It contained an officer, two girls and twenty-three soldiers, all of whom were made to march. Further down the road they encountered an NKA truck bogged in the slush. Mistaking Larson's party for Russians the North Koreans greeted them warmly, the officer indicating he needed a tow. Larson attempted to take the officer's pistol and he let out a yell, causing the Koreans to disappear into the dark.

The CO of the Argylls, Lt Col Neilson, and his 2iC, Maj Sloane, were forced to hide during the night when they drove into a battalion of North Koreans.[3]

At about this time we adopted the American three-stage rationing system, A, B and C rations. "C" ration (Combat Ration) was a one-day ration pack for one man, containing three canned meals, cracker biscuits, coffee, sugar, margarine, jam, cigarettes and toilet paper. "B" ration was larger tins of canned meat, vegetables and other items and was meant to be prepared in a field kitchen for a whole company or by troops in small detachments with cooking facilities. "A" ration was fresh food, which we rarely saw and then only in reserve areas.

An action on the 18th was typical for the pursuit operation. A Company under Maj (Speed) Gordon was leading the battalion en route for Samgapo, mounted on Sherman tanks. Approaching Samgapo they drew fire from the village. The tanks responded with .50cal machine guns and their 9pdr main armaments. A Company dismounted, lined up and attacked through the village. This action killed five of the enemy and three were captured. A Company had no casualties.[4]

Northward movement continued until the 20th when we reached the outskirts of Pyongyang, the capital of North Korea. Here 27 BCB was held back, while 1 Cavalry Division and every press correspondent in theatre entered the city. The Americans were always reluctant to share credits with other forces. US 24 Division was to take over the chase with 27 BCB brigade under command. However, this Division was well to the rear and would take some time to come forward, so 27 BCB was tasked to lead off again.

Also on the 20th, the US 187 Airborne Regimental Combat Team (RCT) was dropped behind enemy lines at Sukchon and Sunchon to cut off the enemy's retreat. (An American regiment is similar to our brigade, having three infantry battalions.) Finding no enemy the Airborne Regiment set out to return to Pyongyang. Their 3 AB Battalion was diverted to check out the town of Yongju on the way. 3 AB Battalion arrived just north of Yongju where they met a North Korean regiment desperately intent on reaching the safety of the north. Finding the AB battalion blocking their escape they attacked the Americans, who retreated, putting out an urgent cry for help. The nearest allied troops were 27th BCB and they got the task. The Argylls led out on the 21st and on reaching Yongju found the North Koreans in occupation and attacked them. With the Argylls ("Jocks") pressing their rear the North Koreans fled north but again found the unfortunate AB Battalion in its path. The North Korean regiment launched another attack on the battalion, which retreated again, with another desperate call for help.

On the 22nd 3 RAR led out to relieve the US troops, but Green had a problem. Apparently the Americans could not give their position with any acceptable degree of accuracy. This situation dictated careful feeling forward to locate enemy and friendly troops. Artillery or mortars could not be employed for fear of shelling the Americans.

Lt Col Green halted 3 RAR on the edge of a large apple orchard, a location he considered a good starting point for searching forward to locate the US formation and the enemy attacking them. Here he assembled the commanders to issue orders for deployment. During Orders it became painfully obvious that Tac HQ had driven into the fringe of the enemy lines. Every few minutes Green would be interrupted by bursts of firing, as the Regimental Police and other HQ security personnel flushed out pockets of the enemy found in the vicinity. Having located the enemy Green now knew that the Americans had to be beyond them. He decided to launch an attack while he had the North Korean Force wrong-footed, and before their commander could reorganise to meet the threat presented by the Australian battalion. The following action became known as the Apple Orchard Battle.

The attack was an unqualified success. C and D companies assaulted in extended line, shooting and bayonetting their way through the North Korean regiment until they surged into the 187 Airborne lines. In this action 150 enemy were killed, 239 wounded and 200 taken prisoner.[5] This battle was important for the battalion, being its first real opportunity to demonstrate its capacity to deal decisively with a numerically superior, organised enemy. Success was due to two factors: Charlie

Green's decision to seize the initiative and launch an immediate attack and the fighting spirit of the Australian Digger to carry it off. The Brits and the Jocks observed the action, curious to see how the Diggers would handle themselves. They were not disappointed. It was our coming of age. Brig Coad described part of the action:

> ... they [the enemy] got down into the paddy and were hiding in the paddy, in the ditches, everywhere sniping and being an infernal nuisance. Then I saw a marvellous sight. An Australian platoon lined up in a paddy field and walked through it as though they were driving snipe. The soldiers, when they saw a pile of straw, kicked it and out would bolt a North Korean. Up with a rifle, down with a North Korean.

The pursuit operation continued until 25 October when the leading elements of the battalion reached Kujin. Here the road turned west across the Taeryong River. The large concrete bridge spanning it had been demolished and rendered impassable to transport, but it was possible to clamber across it on foot. Lt Alby Morrison and two sections of his 4 Platoon made it over and on the far bank were confronted by about fifty enemy, hands in the air. Morrison encouraged them to come down, but another enemy group, hidden in the shrub higher up, opened fire as they approached. By this time the Air Contact Team (ACT) spotter aircraft had reported two company of enemy in close proximity to 4 Platoon, and Lt Col Green ordered Morrison to withdraw. The platoon returned successfully, bringing ten prisoners with them.[6]

D Company under Wally Brown had been dispatched to clear the town of Pakchon. They returned with 225 prisoners, having left a platoon to guard a US Combat Engineer outfit building a ford over the Taeryong river.

It was approaching dusk and Green had to make a bold tactical decision. He could proceed via the ford the next day or attempt a lodgement that night. He decided not to give the enemy a chance to set up defence on the opposite bank and to go with a night operation.

Lt Col Green ordered an air strike on the ridges

immediately across the river and followed this up with mortar and artillery barrages. He then pushed A and B companies across, one on each side of the road.

It was not long before B Company began to get enemy attention. A group of about company strength with tanks began forming up on their front. Artillery and mortar fire disrupted the attack and it was held off by the Diggers. Two enemy T34 tanks shelled and machine-gunned B Company. The tanks were obviously unaware of B Company's actual location, as one of them approached and halted within ten metres of company headquarters. They fired blindly on B Company and across the river at Battalion Headquarters, but without any effect. On arrival in Korea the battalion had been equipped with new US 3.5 anti-tank Bazookas, but try as they might, our operators could not get them to fire at these sitting-duck targets.

Enemy artillery ranged in on the companies and Battalion Headquarters but fortunately none of the shells exploded on impact. They were possibly armour piercing ammunition from an anti tank gun, or HE not properly armed.

During the night enemy attacks on B Company increased, with enemy groups being broken up by defensive fire tasks from artillery and mortars. Lt Colin Townsend's 8 Platoon was sent from A Company to reinforce B Company.

At 0400 hours on the 26th A Company became aware of a force of infantry and tanks moving towards them. In addition to the tanks there were two Russian jeeps, a motorcycle and about sixty troops which approached, obviously unaware we had troops on that side of the bridge. A Company let them come on until they were right under their defences, then opened up, with devastating effect. The enemy fled in panic, leaving the vehicles behind. A Company scored one of the Russian jeeps, which remained part of its Fighting Echelon transport for many months to come. The transport won the motorcycle for the dispatch riders.

The battalion casualties for this action were eight killed and twenty-two wounded, the killed including Lt Joppy Wathen of A Company. On the enemy side, there were over 100 dead.

This action became known as the Broken Bridge defence.

On 27 and 28 October 1 Middlesex and 1 A&SH took the lead against little opposition. However, the reintroduction of artillery and tanks into the enemy operations indicated stiffening of resistance as the allies approached the Chinese border. This was confirmed on the 29th when 3 RAR continued the advance to Chongju.

As D Company approached Chongju on the left of the road, Mosquito spotter aircraft reported that enemy tanks and infantry were on a ridge forward of the battalion. Lt Col Green laid on air strikes and artillery to soften up the enemy before committing D Company to the attack. The US Air Force reported knocking out all the tanks, but this proved to be a gross over-estimation.

Supported by tanks, D Company attacked against determined resistance and gained the objective by 1630 hours.

On the other side of the road, A Company, now under the command of Capt Bill Chitts,[7] attacked, supported by tanks. They also met determined resistance, but by 1730 had taken their objective. During the day the platoons destroyed eleven Russian T34 tanks and two SU76 SP guns with bazooka fire. Pte Stafford destroyed one tank with his Bren gun, by setting fire to the auxiliary fuel tank strapped to it.[8]

At 2000 hours the enemy counter-attacked D Company in strength, in the area of Lt Dave Mannett's 10 Platoon. The enemy drove in with determination, wave upon wave, but 10 Platoon beat off the assaults, giving no ground, although the enemy managed to get on to their rear.

At 2130 hours a desperation, screaming, Banzi-type attack was launched against A Company. The company held firm and the platoons, supported by artillery and mortar fire, fought it off. In the morning 150 enemy dead were counted in front of the 3 RAR defences. The battalion's casualties were nine killed and thirty wounded. Charlie Green was obviously pleased with the unit's aggressive execution of the attacks and subsequent stolid defence, for he was heard to remark: "They can send them on by divisions now; this battalion will accommodate them."

The 1 Cavalry Division Commander, Gen Hobart Gay, was also impressed by the Chongju result. He sent Brig Coad a signal:

> Congratulations on your splendid and sensational drive into enemy territory. I know it is a proud day in your brigade's record and one which deserves the envy of all soldiers. I send my sincerest congratulations and commendations to you and all the officers and men of the Argyll and Sutherland Highlanders, the Middlesex Regiment and 3rd Battalion of the Royal Australian Regiment, who marched 31 miles in twelve hours to deal the enemy this disastrous blow.

Green was ordered to take another feature forward of Chongju. This was gained without firing a shot and the battalion dug in in defence.

Within the 3rd Battalion mutual confidence had developed through the dramatic victories of the Apple Orchard, Broken Bridge and Chongju. The battalion's success was a combination of Charlie Green's fine leadership and the aggressive professionalism of the Digger. Green was taciturn by nature, communicating little of his inner feelings, but this did not prevent him from gaining the full confidence of both the officers and the men. He had a sound tactical sense combined with an infallible ability to relate map to ground. His orders were clear and concise, leaving no doubt of what was to be achieved. All Green's actions were immediate attacks, coming straight off the line of march. He was never presented with an opportunity for the carefully prepared set-piece battle. By the end of October unit morale had developed to the extent that 3 RAR was prepared to take on all comers, and give away a pound or two if necessary.

There is a fatalistic axiom among soldiers, that if your name is on a bullet or shell, it will seek you out. On the afternoon of 30 October 1950 thirty-four members of 3 RAR headquarters were bustling about the business of setting up and digging in for the night. On the ridge above them an enemy high velocity gun was firing at the rifle company consolidating on it. Some shells went whistling overhead, some bounced off the ridge to tumble over and over into the fields beyond. Although he had not slept for thirty-six hours, Lt Col Charlie Green did his rounds of the companies prior to retiring to his tent to rest. A vagrant shell tumbled into a tree at the foot of the re-entrant where the headquarters were located. It exploded, sending a large fragment of shrapnel through the CO's tent which ripped open his stomach. The wound proved fatal. Of the thirty or so soldiers in that confined space, the shell selected but one victim. C 'est la Guerre.

TWO

THE BATTLE OF PAKCHON

Colonel Green was wounded on 30 October 1950 and died two days later, his death coinciding with the opening of the Chinese Army First Phase Offensive. The replacement for Charlie Green was not the 2iC, Maj I. B. Ferguson, as expected, but Lt Col F. S. Walsh, the man who had commanded 3 RAR during the occupation of Japan but had been overlooked as Commanding Officer in Korea. Now, less than two months later, Walsh was ordered to resume command of the battalion. In Walsh's words:

> The Chief of Staff warned me that Charles Green was badly wounded, as he was at that stage, and Robbie (Lt Gen H. C. H. Robertson) wanted me to go up and take temporary command because he thought there might be some loss of morale and the battalion would be shocked by the death of the commander and also because I knew the battalion from Japan.[1]

For the North Korean Army, the battle at Chongju had been a last ditch stand. With its capture the road was open for a clear chase to the Manchurian border, with no features suitable for the North Korean Army to again take up a serious defensive position. From our location in reserve outside Chongju we witnessed US Army 24 Division pouring north unopposed, to keep a photographic appointment with the press, at the border with China, the Yalu River. Reports of Chinese formations making hostile forays were ignored until 3 and 4 November. It then became abundantly clear that the Chinese Communist Forces were deep into Korea in great strength and with very hostile intentions. The US Army divisions which motored north so enthusiastically a few days previously now scampered south with all the speed their motor battalions could muster. Having no troop-carrying capacity of its own, the Commonwealth Brigade could not join in this southward excursion. It was completely dependent on the US Army for mobility and they were not sharing resources at a time like this.

The Brigade was moved to the vicinity of Pakchon on the west side of the Taeryong River, as a rear guard to cover the withdrawing US Divisions and to await further developments.

The Chinese Communist Forces were to sort out this situation for us on the night of 4 November. Swooping from out of nowhere they attacked a battery of US 61st Artillery Battalion, situated astride the road blocking the 27 BCB withdrawal route. A company of the Argyll and Sutherland Highlanders with four tanks was ordered to clear the road. This company was commanded by David Wilson, always recognisable by a hunting horn slung over one shoulder. David described the scene which greeted them as they approached the battle area:

> Captain Howard M. More formed his six guns into a semicircle and engaged the enemy over open sights at almost point blank range. In older days he would have had what we called "canister" but instead he depressed his guns so that the shells bounced off the frozen paddy and exploded in the enemy's faces. As we arrived, we could see his gunners being shot up behind their gun shields while others took their place. It was like seeing something from a war in the Napoleonic Area.[2]

With a blast from David's horn the tanks and Jocks charged the Chinese, driving them back to a hill about five hundred metres east of the road. From this position the Chinese still dominated the brigade withdrawal route, so the horn blasted again, and Wilson's men attacked, sending the enemy running. However, they did not run far enough. Pausing to reorganise, they counter-attacked in strength, forcing the Jocks to pull off their feature to be pinned down on a reverse slope, guarding their dead and wounded. At this stage 3 RAR was ordered to attack and recover the dominating crests.

The feature occupied by the Chinese was a ridge on the east of the road and about five hundred metres from it. There were three main crests on the ridge running in a south-easterly direction, the first nearest the road, the second close behind it and a third further back. The Chinese occupied the first two crests. The CO allocated the first crest as the A Company objective (under Capt Bill Chitts), the second to B Company (under Capt Darcy Laughlin), ordering them to put their heads together to work out how they were going to do it. Using the road as a start line, the companies had an approach of about five hundred metres of open paddy field to cover to reach the first (A Company) objective. The Chinese had already arranged that there should be no artillery support available, but a program for the 3 inch Mortar and MMG platoons was registered.

The Mustangs of RAAF 77 Fighter Squadron chose this moment to provide a boost to morale by bursting on to the scene, strafing the enemy positions — the first time they had been able to support us.

With bayonets fixed and in extended line, both companies crossed the start line, A Company on the left and B Company on the right. The companies drew enemy fire immediately from machine guns and mortars, causing early casualties. On arrival at the bottom of its objective A Company liberated the Jocks, then charged up the slope and with bayonet and bullet thrashed the enemy off the feature. This set up the situation for B Company, which took the second crest with equal enthusiasm, but among their casualties was the popular and respected Lt Eric Larson, who was killed. Both companies made preparations to stand off the inevitable counter-attack. As expected, the companies received considerable attention from enemy machine guns and mortars, one mortar bomb landing on A Company headquarters, severely wounding the OC, Bill Chitts, and killing and wounding other members of his headquarters, including the CSM, "Sticks" McGavin, the radio operator and the orderly. Lt L. G. (Algy) Clark immediately took command of the difficult situation, and the company continued to suffer casualties from a succession of enemy counter-attacks which were being aggressively resisted by the platoons.

With the success of A and B companies, the CO ordered D Company (Maj Wally Brown) to occupy the third crest and C Company (Maj Arch Denness) the paddy fields between A Company and the road.

When advised of success, the brigadier instructed Walsh to consolidate on the captured ground and put troops at the railway bridge below us, where refugees were streaming across. The problem with refugees in the area was the possibility of the enemy from whom they were fleeing mingling with them in the dark to infiltrate to the brigade rear. Walsh considered he did not have the capacity to allocate troops for the bridge and ignored this instruction. From a defence point of view A, B and D companies secured the crests on the battalion's right flank, and the gap between A Company and the road was covered by C Company. The left (west) of the road was guarded by the Taeryong river. With all companies operationally committed there was obviously no reserve.

It was now approaching dusk and the CO instructed me to establish his headquarters west of the road in the area between the river and the road. Setting up headquarters was by now pretty much a routine. Nearest the entrance I sited the Signal Centre, and the RMO, Capt Vardanegar, and his medical facilities were at the exit. In the centre was the CO's tent with the Adjutant, Capt John Callander, and myself nearest it. The Brigade Rear Link communications vehicle and the Intelligence

Officer, Lt Alf Argent, with his Intelligence section close by. On this occasion we had no supporting arms to accommodate. The RSM, WOI Harrison, in conjunction with the Signal Sergeant, Sgt Gallaway, and the Regimental Police organised the defence layout of the HQ. During all of this activity a batch of about twenty reinforcements reported in and to their eloquently expressed disgust were immediately put to work digging weapon pits. By nightfall we had a fully functional headquarters, with line and radio communications established to all companies and the support platoons, the RMO and his staff hard at it preparing casualties for evacuation, and troops disposed in defence of the headquarters. The Brigade HQ Rear Link radio speaker blared out brigade traffic for all throughout the headquarters to hear.

An unfortunate aspect of the headquarters site was its proximity to the Mortar Platoon's base plate position on the opposite side of the road, where they were energetically pumping out bombs in response to Defensive Fire task requests. This, of course, attracted generous Chinese retaliation with mortar and machine gun fire, some of the mortar bombs landing disturbingly close to the headquarters area, although none came in. The enemy mortar fire caused the CO to instruct me to relocate his headquarters a thousand yards to the rear. I protested that to pull down a functioning headquarters in the dark and establish it elsewhere, would be a messy business, particularly from a communications and casualty evacuation point of view. However, he was determined to move, so I told him that as we pulled down the headquarters and loaded vehicles they would be dispatched to the rear, and requested he detail someone to receive and establish them tactically in the new area. Prior to leaving to select the new HQ site the CO contacted the brigadier on the rear link, advising of the enemy counter-attacks in progress, the mortaring and his intention to move headquarters to safer ground. The brigadier's reply was broadcast loud and clear: "If your headquarters is being mortared it may be wise to move it, but the rifle companies must remain in present localities."

In company with the adjutant, the IO and the Brigade Rear link the CO departed and we settled down to the extremely unpopular and confusing task of striking and loading tents and dispatching headquarters vehicles in the dark. The RMO protested the loudest, being heavily involved with attending to casualties in various stages of preparation for evacuation. All I could offer was sympathy, which was not a great help and not cheerfully received. It was three or four in the morning when I followed the last vehicle down the road to the new headquarters site.

I was not so naive as to expect an ideal layout of the headquarters in its new area but was totally unprepared for the utter chaos which greeted me. Absolutely nothing had been done to re-establish the headquarters, four unmanned 17-pounder guns of the Anti-Tank Platoon were strung out along the road, headquarters vehicles remained loaded where they had halted on arrival, and the RMO was treating casualties on the roadside and pushing them up culverts to provide some scant protection from the night air. A sort of ad hoc tactical headquarters had evolved around the brigade rear link vehicle, with a grouping of brigade and battalion command net radios and the headquarters staff standing by (Adjutant, Intelligence Officer and Signals Officer). Absolutely nothing had been done about security and there were groups of soldiers, including the recently arrived reinforcements, standing around waiting for instructions.

The adjutant, Capt John Callander, briefed me on the operational situation so far as he knew it. With the movement of the headquarters the CO had ordered a general withdrawal of all the rifle companies at 2000 hours. This was done without selection of alternative defensive positions, provision for rear reconnaissance, timings, order of company movement or any other planning data. B Company made no immediate move but withdrew later when things settled down. C Company moved as ordered. B and D companies were commanded by AIF veterans with enough experience to handle the situation. A Company, however, was now commanded by a young lieutenant and his company was under attack. He questioned the wisdom of the withdrawal but the order was confirmed, leaving him no option but to comply.[3] The enemy took advantage of the confusion of uncoordinated movement in the dark and cut A Company about badly. Lt Bill Key's platoon came out unscathed but the others and company headquarters drew heavy casualties, including the commander of 2 Platoon, Lt Noel (Chic) Charlesworth, who was wounded.

When the brigadier became aware of the withdrawal he ordered the companies be returned to their original positions. Except for D Company this was now impossible. Even with fresh, full-strength companies the task of mounting an unsupported night attack against a numerically superior enemy, without daylight preparation, would have had a dubious chance of success. With the current strengths, location and condition of A and B companies, night attacking was not a proposition.

D Company commenced withdrawal, but on being ordered to return to their crest did so, and refused to answer any further radio traffic for the remainder of the night.

This was the situation as it appeared to us at this time: We had no idea about D Company, because we had no radio contact with them, but we knew this was simply to avoid further instructions until daylight. Should they get into trouble we would hear about it soon enough. B Company we knew was somewhere in the paddy fields but the exact location was unknown. C Company was repositioned in the paddy fields forward of battalion headquarters. The only information on A Company came from stragglers and casualties but this was all bad news, leading us to suspect that A Company was non-existent, or at best non-effective. Any way we looked at it there was a mighty big gap between D Company and C Company, through which the opposition could march a regiment, wiping out battalion headquarters on its way to brigade. Support Company was under Captain Cyril Hall, who tried to make some sort of order out of the situation that confronted him. He established the mortars where they could provide fire and protected them with the Anti-Tank Platoon gun crews acting as infantry. This accounted for the unmanned anti-tank guns in the middle of the road. At this stage, Cyril said, I then reported to the CO and went off to dig my own "slitty", clean my rifle and prepare to meet my maker, an event I thought would surely follow, come daylight.[4]

The CO appeared at the Rear Link location from time to time and seemed to be conducting the operation from the radio in his jeep. To establish some sort of security I gathered up all unoccupied soldiers in the immediate area and marched them in a semicircle around the headquarters, dropping off a man every few metres with instructions to face outwards and shoot any one who came in his path who did not give the password, or speak like an Australian. Usually if a soldier did not know, or forgot, the password, he let fly with a mouthful of unmistakable barracks invective, thus putting identification beyond all doubt. The password for that night was itself ominous: Acid Bath. We settled down to await what dawn might bring.

Come daylight there was uncanny quiet everywhere. Our enemy had completely disappeared, leaving us to conjecture that he had over extended his administrative capacity to continue the contest. The CO drove off down the road to locate and do something about the rifle companies. The headquarters shambles badly needed sorting out but little could be done until the tactical location of the companies was established. It was then

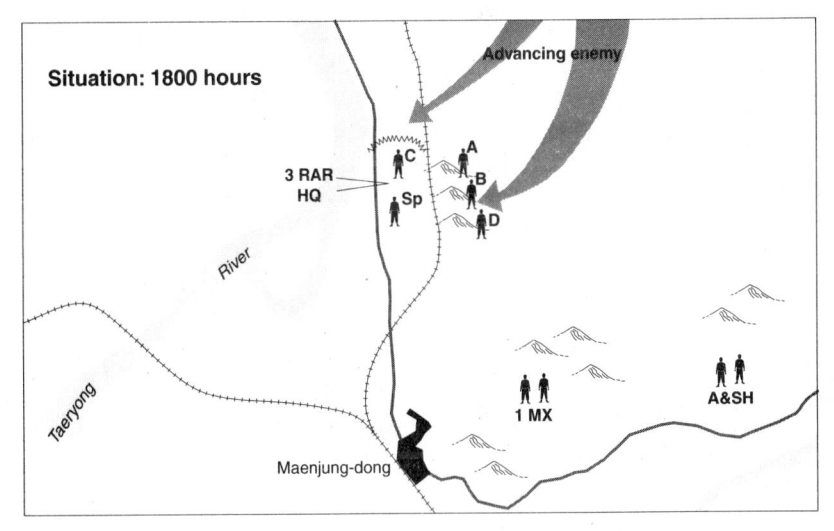

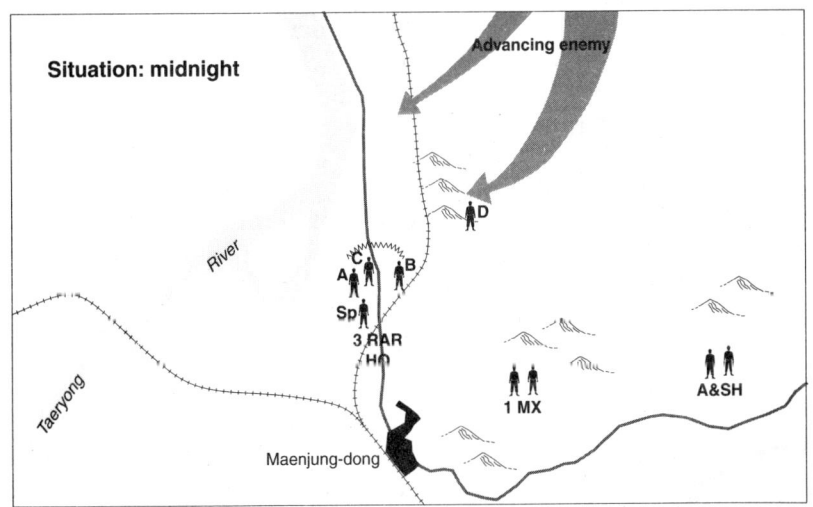

Map 2: Battle of Pakchon, 5–6 November 1950

that the brigadier arrived, looking for the CO. On being informed that he was forward with the companies, the brigadier pushed his map board at me, telling me to indicate the company locations. This was embarrassing. C and D companies were easy enough. The guess about B Company was vague — somewhere behind C Company. But of A Company I could only tell him that they had had a bad night, taking heavy casualties, and until the remnants had been rounded up we could not establish the extent. Then came the thousand-dollar question: what was at the bridge? On being told "nothing" a normally florid visage became dangerously more so: "O'Dowd, I want a company here, here, here and here and when your CO returns tell him I want to see him."

He then departed in the direction of Brigade Headquarters.

The CO returned shortly after and I briefed him on the brigadier's instructions for the location of the companies and informed him that he was required at Brigade. He instructed me to carry on, and immediately disappeared along the road to brigade. At Brigade Headquarters Brig Coad showed Colonel Walsh a signal from General Robertson's Headquarters ordering his return to the staff of Eighth Army Headquarters in Seoul. Then things began to move fast. While we were trying to get a handle on the situation, the 2iC, Maj I. B. Ferguson, arrived, announcing that he was to take command of the battalion. I briefed him on the state of the game and he informed me that he would take over from there. My final task as Battle 2iC was to establish his headquarters on a piece of rising ground to our immediate rear. Then came the good news that I would take over command of the battered A Company, the great band of fighting men that I had the honour to command for the remainder of my tour in Korea.

So ended the Pakchon saga. Until that time, whenever the Chinese attacked, the United Nations forces had withdrawn (or rather bugged out, as the Americans so aptly described the panic process being practised).

Actually attacking the Chinese had not yet been contemplated. A myth of invincibility began to develop around these tough, battle-hardened soldiers who swooped out of the hills and attacked relentlessly without support of air or artillery. However, the Diggers had ignored enemy mortar and machine gun fire, and charged in with bayonet and bullet to drive them from the crests. The enemy had then resorted to the continuous mass attacks we were later to become so familiar with, but this had been met with disciplined aggression and not an inch of ground had been given until the companies' withdrawal had been ordered. The soldiers of 3 RAR in no way let down the reputation of the Regiment. They did all that was asked of them and did it bravely and well.

By midnight the battalion had achieved spectacular success, but by four in the morning it was a bad tactical joke. The aim of the operation was to gain and maintain control of the features dominating the road. This had been achieved then relinquished to the enemy. B and C companies were in a precarious position come daylight, sitting in an exposed paddy field under the guns of the Chinese-held features. D Company was isolated from the remainder of the battalion. A Company was in such a mess it was non-effective. No one really knows why the general withdrawal of the four companies had been ordered, but this most difficult and dangerous phase of war, requiring meticulous planning and careful execution, had been ordered in the dark, with a company under attack and without rear reconnaissance or selection of alternative defensive features.

Pte Vic Carr of 3 Platoon has written an account of the action from the perspective of an A Company Digger:

> It was a time that 7 Section of A Coy of 3 RAR would always remember. On the afternoon of 5th of November 1950, south of Broken Bridge, "Pakchon", RAR was preparing to assault a ridge line held by the Chinese and North Korean forces.
>
> There were also a number of A&SH pinned down at the

foot of the ridge. A and B Coy were ordered to attack in extended line, and after the ridge was taken, C Coy was to take up positions on the flat on A Coy's left, with D Coy in reserve.

On that day 7 Section consisted of Cpl Charlie Scholl, L/Cpl Dave Koonsey, and Ptes Charlie Donovan, Vic Carr, Lofty Maletz, Bobby Wilson, Ray Chilcott, Geoff Butler and Tommy Watson. Next morning only two remained.

The battalion attacked without supporting arms (i.e. artillery) but we moved, with about 800 yards of open ground to reach the foothills. Mustangs from 77Sqn RAAF roared overhead to strafe enemy positions, as we came under machine gun fire which was quite heavy.

One of the first casualties was Mick Servos of A Coy from 2 Platoon. George Cape, 3 Platoon HQ was hit and came across to his mate and called out, "I'm hit, Charlie."

Donovan said, "Piss off, George, you'll draw the crabs."

George said, "I've been hit in the heart."

Donovan said, "Don't be bloody silly, you are not dead yet."

A Company took some casualties from heavy machine gun fire, but having made the foothills, passed through the A&SH and started to get on with the job of taking the ridge line.

As we neared the summit a large number of mortar bombs fell among A Coy wounding quite a few, including Coy Commander Bill Chitts. Word came along: "Bill Chitts hit in the legs". Reply came back: "Don't be silly, haven't you seen him in shorts". One mortar bomb fell among 7 Section, and badly wounded Ray Chilcott, Tommy Watson and Geof Butler, and while Bobby Wilson and I [Vic Carr] were putting out the fires (clothes were burning) and trying to give comfort, Bobby Wilson spun round — he had been hit in the elbow.

Platoon Commander Chic Charlesworth ordered us to leave the wounded for the stretcher bearers and continue the attack.

We finally took the ridge line and set up a defensive position on the forward slopes, also taking stock of casualties. Of 7 Section, only three remained (Scholl, Maletz and Carr). Koonsey was killed; Wilson, Chilcott, Butler, Donovan and Watson were wounded. A Coy set about digging. 7 Section, down to three men, had one man to each hole instead of two. All of A Company were thin on the ground.

Late that night we could hear the enemy moving about and shots were being exchanged. Sometime later Fred Origlassie from 8 Section was crouched down telling me to get my gear ready to move out, when the angry man fired and killed Fred. Finally we were ordered to withdraw, and while approaching one platoon position we were met with a hail of fire and showers of grenades. We were calling for them to stop firing.

I can recall Shorty Mavin calling them bloody noggies.[5] Chic Charlesworth had been hit. It was dark and we were getting confused, then we realised it was the Chinese who were shooting at us, so we went back down the forward slopes. Our group consisted of about six men, which included 3Pl Sgt Knoggie Beavis, 7 Section Maletz and three others, all wounded. Beavis said to me, "Vic, you are the only one of us not hit, you will have to lead us out." After a few hours, passing through a burning village, we must have passed behind B Coy and forward of D Coy. We crossed over a saddle and down the flat and stumbled around in the dark. We finally found the road we had started from.

We turned south and a few minutes later heard, "Halt. Password." I still remember it today, "Acid Bath". We put the wounded on the tank at the road block, and that left me to find the battalion. Next morning as day broke, striding across the paddy field was that familiar figure, Charlie Scholl. All I could say was, "I've still got your watch, Charlie." I was on picket when the withdrawal started that night. Charlie got hit on Hill 410 later and I was to go full term.

THREE

ASSEMBLING THE TEAM

It was good to be back in a rifle company, having spent the entire World War II, from 1939 until the end, with 2/11th Australian Infantry Battalion. When Charlie Green had brought me into his headquarters as Headquarters Company Commander and Battle 2iC I had been happy to serve in this capacity, but, following his death, I looked forward to returning to my natural environment, a rifle company.

Given a choice of commands it would most certainly have been A Company. Like D Company, these fine men had displayed tremendous fighting spirit in the Chongju attacks and the conduct and courage displayed during the Pakchon battle left no doubts they were a fine nucleus upon which to rebuild a company.

Prior to relinquishing HQ Company, I had an opportunity to study my new command. General attrition plus casualties from the fighting at the Broken Bridge and Chongju and Pakchon had reduced it to a non-battle-worthy state. The only remaining officer was Lt L. G. (Algy) Clark, who had commanded them during the crucial withdrawal stage of Pakchon. There was no Company Sergeant Major, only one platoon sergeant, Sgt Vic Svenson, and a smattering of private soldiers in the platoons. However, the Pakchon debacle had not shaken them, and morale was still high.

I discussed this with Maj Ferguson, who promised first call on reinforcements, officers and other ranks. With this promise went a warning that I should lose no time putting the company together because he intended to task A Company for the first attack. This reasoning was based on the theory that "the best way to restore confidence in a rider who takes a fall, is to put him back in the saddle". I was not too sure how aptly it applied to this situation, but assurance of prompt reinforcement was welcome, and he was to keep his word.

The administrative side of the company was in good shape. The platoon and company headquarters vehicles and drivers were intact, having been sent to the rear before battle was joined. Similarly my Company Quartermaster Sergeant, S/Sgt Crawley, his storeman, Cpl Bill Mann, my company clerk, Cpl Lennie Taylor, and the cooks, Cpl Robinson, Cpl Cliff Muncy and Pte Taylor, were all located safely in B Echelon and fully functional. The personnel shortages were in the all important fighting element, the platoons. I knew that the "other rank" reinforcements would all be K Force privates, which would necessitate platoon commanders making rapid assessments of talent for future leaders.

Fortunately the K Force reinforcements were not wide-eyed, adventure-seeking youths but battle-hardened warriors, previously blooded in World War II. They came from every division in the AIF. Some had fought in the Western Desert, Syria or New Guinea campaigns, and in some cases all of these. This was fine material to build on, men who had already held rank in infantry battalions and were ready to resume the role of section commander or platoon sergeant, when called upon to do so.

Until my arrival Lt Algy Clark had continued in command of A Company, reorganising the remnants into the framework of a rifle company, ready to feed in the K Force reinforcements who had arrived during the fighting on 5 November. At this stage Algy had more intimate knowledge of the platoons than I, so I retained him in the 2iC position and left him to build up the platoons. In mid-November five officers and more other rank reinforcements marched in to the battalion, and A Company's share brought it to full strength.

The new officers were all strangers to me. Lt Reg Saunders I knew by reputation only. He was the first (and, at that stage, only) Aborigine to hold a King's Commission. During the New Guinea campaigns this precedent had received considerable publicity. I assumed he had had exceptional operational leadership to make such a breakthrough in 2/7th Australian Infantry Battalion. Nevertheless I was curious as to how the company would react to an Aboriginal commander. I gave him 1 Platoon where Vic Svenson was the Platoon Sergeant, and from the beginning there was no doubt he was held in high regard and accepted as their leader. It was as it should have been.

2 Platoon went to Teddy Beacroft but he did not last long. His artillery background saw him reposted to the 17 pounder Anti-Tank Platoon. Command of 2 Platoon reverted to the Platoon Sergeant, Sgt George Harris, who fortuitously returned from hospital the same day Beacroft was transferred out, 20 November 1950. George was an aggressive leader, destined to take over command of this platoon on more than one occasion.

Lt Harold Mulry was 3 Platoon commander. He worried me at first, looking a bit long in the tooth for the job. Platoon commanders usually came in their early twenties, whereas I was thirty-three and Harold was three years older than I. However, he proved to be a rugged individual, sincerely religious, a non-smoker and non-drinker who frowned on bad language. Harold wouldn't use a vulgar fraction. He had left a happy marriage and family and a steady job in Cairns to voluntarily fight in this war. When asked what in hell he was doing in Korea, his reply was simple: "Communism is an evil thing and we have a duty to fight it."

He had to be the only man in Korea with such pure

motivation. And fight Communism he did! His day was made any time 3 Platoon was tasked to lead an attack or take off into the blue on a nasty patrol. With total confidence I knew this platoon would hit hard. Harold was a splendid leader, and his men had tremendous respect for him and absolute confidence in his leadership. Any company commander with a Harold Mulry has indeed been blessed.

My forward headquarters was rebuilt from reinforcements plus attachments from Headquarters and Support companies. I acquired two good signallers, Brian (Lofty) Heweston and Horace (Slim) Madden.[1] Slim should not have been in a rifle company, being a linesman, not a radio operator, but nevertheless he gave good support to Lofty. Heweston always managed to coax transmission from the 22 and 128 radio sets we were issued with at that time.

My driver was Pte Dave Smith, known by one and all as Smiffy, a rough diamond with a dry sense of humour, reflecting an upbringing in the school of hard knocks. Early in the piece he guaranteed that my jeep would always be in good running order, and commence the day with a full tank of petrol and an equally full spare jerry can on the back. Smiffy never let me down. He could take that jeep uphill, through mud, and maintain an even keel on treacherous ice-bound roads.

Smiffy's regimental number should have been 3400001, marking him as the number one K Force enlistee for Victoria. Determined not to miss out on K Force, he parked himself outside the recruiting centre at three in the morning. Towards opening time the press arrived to interview recruit number one, subjecting Smiffy to questioning and having him pose for photographs. As the doors opened Smiffy was asked for just one more photograph. He obliged and hastened to the reporting desk, to discover that there were now fourteen men queued in front of him. He became 3400015. The price of fame.

In operational situations a company commander was not in a position to tend to his own protection. His attention was fully occupied keeping track of the changing tactical situation, communicating on the company and command radio nets, and directing support fire. In any case he had only a .38 revolver, carried for cosmetic purposes. It was essential, therefore, that he had an orderly at his side, armed with a sub-machine gun. I instructed a platoon commander to provide me with such a man, and he came up with Pte Roy Nunan. I don't think he parted with one of his treasures.

My first impressions were not good and familiarity improved them but little. Nevertheless, Nunan was a loyal individual who grew on me, and I kept him under my wing. In trying to get close to this soldier I discovered he came from Newtown, a suburb of Sydney, which at that time had a rather indifferent reputation. I gained the impression that there were two guiding influences on his upbringing — his Catholic mother of whom he always spoke with affection, and a very large local policeman of whom he didn't. The policeman belonged to the old school of local cop, and dealt out summary punishment to young men in preference to arrest and the beginning of a criminal record. This policeman's height and size had earned him the sobriquet of Long Tac Sam, after a pre-war heavyweight wrestler of that name. Nunan described this policeman's modus operandi:

"Boss, I am just standing outside this dance hall an' along comes this Long Tac Sam."
"Go home, Nunan."
"You can't tell me to go home."
"Go home, Nunan."
"I ain't doin' nothin'."
"Go home, Nunan."
"I'm just standin' here mindin' my own business."
"GO HOME NUNAN !!"
"Well, I started walking, Boss, an' after about ten minutes I turn an' yell, "Get Stuffed!"

He takes two strides and kicks me right up the arse. He was a terrible big man, Boss."

Something had to be done about a Company Sergeant Major. I rather anticipated we would not have disciplinary problems so was not looking for a shouter and screamer, the traditional image attending this appointment. Discipline through charge reports is a poor form of leadership, and as it turned out it was never necessary to place a man on a charge report while in the company. I was looking for someone who could be relied upon. Someone with a strength of character and personality to get things done with the minimum of fuss. He would be responsible for discipline generally and take control of the headquarters personnel and its security. He would also be responsible for ammunition supply. At this stage I had two sergeants, Vic Svenson and George Harris, one of whom should logically have been given the job. However, both were somewhat strangers to me. The Mortar Platoon had attached Sgt Tom Muggleton to the company as our Mobile Fire Controller (MFC). Tom I knew well from the Japanese Occupation days. He was fit and tough, the captain of our rugby team in Japan. But apart from that he had a cool head and was respected as a reliable sergeant. All things considered I reckoned we would not do better than Muggleton. There was a problem, though. As a Mortar Platoon man he was Support Company property, and they would not surrender him easily. A strong case was put to the CO who, fortunately, ruled in our favour. There were never any regrets about that decision. It was indeed a fortunate day we acquired Muggleton for our Company Sergeant Major.

The rule was that reinforcements marched in as private soldiers. Occasionally the Reinforcement Holding Unit (RHU) created a temporary sergeant or corporal to assist with movement of the draft to Korea, and he would be busted to private immediately on allocation to a company. Section leaders were chosen from battle proven members. A reinforcement draft came to us under such a sergeant and when the handing-over process was done, I told him to take the stripes off his arm. He responded that he could not be busted because he held substantive rank. If true, this put him beyond my prerogative to reduce him. I questioned him closely concerning the circumstances surrounding this precedent and was advised he held a King's Commission, having graduated from Sandhurst in the UK before being sent to the North West Frontier in India where he was decorated with an MC. During World War II he became an RAF pilot, and was decorated with two DFCs and a DCM. Furthermore, he had spent a period as a guest of Mr Hitler, when shot down over Germany.

This was a worry, because the men preferred section leaders to come from their battle-proven mates. Asking them to go into battle under an unproven, non-infantry stranger would not go over well. Although a very presentable, well-spoken fellow, who could quite possibly have held a commission, I did not believe his story. I told the CO I suspected he was an impostor and requested a check be run on him. Meanwhile he had to go to a platoon, and as 3 Platoon had no sergeant Harold Mulry won him. A few days later I found that someone had blackened one of his eyes, and on inquiry was informed he was not fitting in. Conscious that some of our young gentlemen played rough, I packed him off to Battalion HQ, with advice he should be employed elsewhere, before real damage was done. It later transpired that he had been an LAC in an RAAF ground crew in South Australia and had never left Australia. He had been around the RAAF long enough to talk convincingly and technically about fighter aircraft, and pick up some good fighter pilot stories. His claim to substantive rank proved untrue, but he finished his time in Korea and, I believe, turned out to be a reasonable Lance Corporal with HQ Company.

Some time later I met a sergeant who had been in the

Reinforcement Holding Unit (RHU) ex-hospital, who had another story about our intrepid RAF pilot.

The OC of RHU was most impressed at having a World War II Battle of Britain hero on strength, but was concerned that his quartermaster could not come up with the appropriate medal ribbons for such a gallant RAF officer. A sergeant was tasked to escort our friend to the Iwakuni RAAF Base, where the deficiency could be corrected. The RAAF officers were also impressed by our hero's stories, and wined and dined him in the Officers' Mess. Well into the night the sounds of gaiety were heard as our hero was regally entertained.

It was not long before we had a full-strength rifle company, but we had little idea how it would perform in the confusion of battle. Four of the five officers, including me, were newly posted in. A large portion of the reinforcement "other ranks" were scattered among the survivors of the Pakchon battle. I was in much the same predicament as Lt Col Charles Green when he took his battalion to Korea. I had watched as Green had grasped every opportunity to exercise sub-units on any minor operation that came along, the companies gaining cohesion and confidence along the way. It gave him a good idea of the qualities of the commanders and men. I looked for similar opportunities.

I prayed for a few cardboard pushovers to come our way before we got a big one. Something my officers and their platoons could to cut their teeth on. A period of "running in".

FOUR

THE RUNNING-IN PHASE

With the company at fighting strength we took up our sector of the defence in the Pakchon area, dug in and commenced the routine of local patrolling. This did not last long, as the Brigade commenced moving north again, seeking out the elusive Chinese Army. Gen MacArthur was convinced that the October–November forays were all the enemy had, and now we could resume the offensive, finish them off and "be home by Christmas". MacArthur was strong on ego and optimism but weak in military intelligence. Like a team of busy ants the Chinese were covertly wending their way down the central spine of North Korea, and, in our sector, were preparing to emerge with guns blazing in the rear of 24th US Division, the formation to which we were attached. However, at this time we were going calmly about our business, happily unaware of the impending disaster.

During the second week in November the CO ordered A Company on to a feature not far from the site of the Pakchon battle. He did not consider it was occupied, but advised me not to take that for granted, as groups of bypassed enemy were known to be wandering about in the general area. From my point of view this represented an ideal opportunity to shake the platoons out in an attack situation. The company halted short of the objective, where I did a quick reconnaissance. There were no obvious signs of enemy occupation, and the forward slopes offered room to deploy a two up with one in reserve formation, giving everyone a guernsey.

I held my first Orders Group (O Gp) being careful to stay strictly with the standard procedure. After allowing enough time for information to filter down to the men, we advanced up the hill in attack formation. Control was by the old World War II SCR536, (walkie-talkie) radio, and we maintained contact as the advance progressed. The line held straight and the pace even until we arrived on the objective, unopposed. It was a good training workout and I felt a lot happier for it. Clearing patrols were dispatched while weapon pits went down and packs and sleeping gear came forward — a practice run at the standard consolidation routine, to be repeated many, many times thereafter.

In mid-November we got a taste of what the Korean winter could do. We had our first snow, and though the days were clear and sunny they were short, and come dusk the temperature plummeted rapidly to freezing point. Each man carried a tent half, so two men could combine to construct a small shelter in rear of their weapon pit. At this stage we had been issued with an American sleeping bag but not the warm inner lining. This made it necessary to carry blankets, making the packs heavy and cumbersome. Our leather boots got wet by day and turned into ice blocks during the night, giving cause to look forward to the issue of American waterproofs. Our World War II jackets, with open flap outside the trousers, were designed to let the air circulate around the body. In these freezing conditions, circulation we could do without. The British jacket belted in at the waist to overcome the problem and the US Army "dry cold" clothing had been designed to preserve body temperature. It was some time before we obtained such sophisticated niceties. The Australian Army had suffered from precisely the same problem in World War II when we were working in the snow in Syria, digging defences on the Lebanon Ranges. During the Occupation of Japan we again experienced freezing conditions in their winter snow period. We are very slow learners when change involves spending defence money on creature comforts.

In general, our soldiers were grossly inexperienced for what was about to be inflicted upon them. The Digger was well versed at survival in desert warfare and had learned to handle the many difficulties of tropical warfare, living and fighting in the jungle. But he had not been conditioned to live and fight in the sub-zero conditions of Korea. He had not been schooled in protecting himself from frostbite and the effect of below-zero temperatures. He had to learn the hard way how to maintain weapons and prevent firing mechanisms from freezing up.

Not having anti-freeze for the radiators brought on a spate of cracked cylinder heads. Fortunately I had done a stint as Transport Officer in Japan during their winter. To overcome the problem there I had rostered drivers to start up and run motors at set periods during the night to keep them warm. At the onset of cold weather in Korea I instituted the same procedure for the company vehicles, and maintained it until reliable anti-freeze fluid became available.

The company was on the ridge for about a week and began to show signs of cohesion. Each day section-strength patrols were dispatched in all directions, searching for any enemy stragglers still in our area. This was good stuff. It gave section commanders an opportunity to establish their authority out in the field, in circumstances offering the possibility of enemy contact. It gave them a good look at their sections at work, helping to assess their strengths and weaknesses.

In this period I came to a working agreement with my cooks. In the Middle East and New Guinea we had been subjected to unavoidably long periods on iron rations — bully beef and tough army biscuits (desert creams) — but whenever possible our cooks brewed up a hot stew. They could make a stew out of anything to hand — tinned meat and vegetables (M & V), bully beef, canned vegetables, spam, anything that came out wet and hot — and the change made for a much happier bunch of Diggers. I was determined we would have hot meals whenever not actually in combat. Therefore I did not react very kindly when informed that the cooks were having some technical problems preparing their hot gastronomical delights, and cold hard rations were a la carte. My immediate reaction was concern for the poor cooks, bored stiff idling their time away with no culinary challenge. I instructed them to bring their rifles and sleeping gear up the hill, dig weapon pits and join in the general fun of operational routine. Fortunately this proved unnecessary, as they discovered a way of overcoming the heating problem, and the subject never arose again.

As it happened, we had a first class team of cooks under Cpl Robinson's supervision. One of them, Cliff Muncy, was a graduate of the William Anglis School of Food Technology and had at one time been a chef at the Naval and Military Club in Melbourne. On occasions when in reserve, I entertained officers from other companies or the Argyll and Sutherland Highlanders. With a bottle of gin my cooks could bribe first class ingredients out of a local Yank supply outfit, and lay on a fine feast. This sort of thing was frowned upon in high places but, like Schultz in the American POW sitcom, "I didn't see nuttin'."

Having our catering staff in good working order soon became a necessity. It transpired there were a number of recently deserted villages on the routes of the daily patrols. With their task complete, they would set the return journey to pass through one of these villages, gathering wandering poultry, the odd baby pig, potatoes, cabbage, onions and whatever other fresh edibles were available. All of this went to the cooks to supplement the rations, and they turned out first class stews. We never got it so good again.

War is about killing, but like everything else it has rules, one being that you do not kill an unarmed enemy who is at your mercy. One day a patrol returned with a young wounded Chinese soldier on an improvised stretcher. He had obviously been exposed for some days and was in poor shape. The Chinese were usually meticulous about evacuation of their wounded from the battlefield, and their dead too, where possible. This unfortunate man must have been overlooked during a night action. I had him transferred to one of our stretchers, and instructed a platoon commander to task a section to carry him to the Regimental Aid Post. He came back with a problem. The section commander concerned was giving trouble, claiming he did not join up to carry "Noggies"[1] around. I told him he had enlisted to do what he was told, and to get on with it. I thought the argument had ended there, but the message got back to me that the corporal was predicting the early demise of the prisoner not far down the track. I did not believe this good NCO would stoop to cold-blooded murder or that the men in the section would stand by while it happened. Nevertheless, it seemed like a good time to enunciate policy. I advised the corporal that if the wounded Chinese was not alive on arrival at battalion headquarters I would personally see to it he went for a court martial. There was never any further trouble of this kind.

In mid-November the battalion moved north again to take up defences along the Taeryong River. The area allocated to A Company was ideal from a defence point of view. From the river a steep, almost vertical, escarpment rose to the crest, offering a field of view for a kilometre or so to the north. With the platoons dug in it was the sort of situation where one might beg the opposition to have a go. My headquarters were located on the reverse slope, along with my HQ tent.

Here the battalion became involved in wide-ranging platoon-strength fighting patrols, and A Company got its share. These were tremendous for running in procedure. Not only did they provide the platoon commanders an opportunity to stamp their authority on the section commanders and troops, but they also gave them practice in tactical handling. Spice was added to these operations by confirmed reports of groups of cut-off, armed enemy wandering in the area, offering the chance of a fight around any corner. Over the next two weeks enemy contacts were not rare. Reg Saunders's 1 Platoon, for instance, with 3 inch mortars and MMG support, was ordered on a fighting patrol. They were tasked to sweep through territory well north of the battalion to search out and kill any enemy encountered. During the day a large group of the enemy was sighted and immediately Reg's men went to work on them, with machine gun and rifle fire, killing seven.[2] The outcome was the enemy taking to the hills with all the speed terrified men can muster. Unfortunately, Saunders patrol was destined for another fire fight on the return journey, this time with friendly troops. A company of ROK soldiers had strayed into our territory and, mistaking 1 Platoon for the enemy, opened fire. Reg's men obliged them instinctively, causing casualties among the South Korean soldiers before mutual recognition ended the unfortunate affair. One of our soldiers was wounded.

Naturally I took a keen interest in the performance of the platoon commanders on these forays, and was gratified to find that the three of them conducted themselves with enthusiasm and credit.

We were issued with US Army shoe packs and field jackets, as yet without the warm inner-pile lining attachment. The jacket lining and pile caps with ear protection were to come forward later. However, when we did get the pile caps it necessary to ban the Diggers from using the protecting ear flaps. They deadened sound, and it was vital that soldiers heard orders clearly, without the necessity to shout.

The advantage of being on US rations was especially

evident when the Americans' special days came around. Thanksgiving Day brought turkey, ham and an assortment of unexpected goodies onto the menu, giving our cooks the opportunity to exercise some ingenuity in preparing them.

The days were still sunny and pleasant but unfortunately they were becoming shorter, and the nights brought extremes of cold that the Diggers were not used to and had to learn to cope with. At morning "stand to" the Bren gunners set the machine guns in position, but left skin and flesh behind on the frozen metal parts. The gunners were eventually issued with lined gloves, minus the trigger finger. During the night the soldiers slept with their automatic weapons, to keep the moving parts from freezing.

During November a number of our junior officers were withdrawn to Australia to assist with the first attempt at National Service. To this cause I lost my 2iC, Algy Clark, with instructions from the CO to replace him from my own resources. I really knew very little about my two lieutenants, so I fell back on the established army seniority system. Reg Saunders was the senior, so he got the promotion.

Next morning I paid a visit to 1 Platoon to advise Reg of his change of status. Finding no evidence of him, I requested direction from one of his Diggers, who indicated a weapon pit. Sure enough there was Saunders, fast asleep at eight o'clock in the morning! I leaned down and put an army boot on his midriff. A big black head emerged from the blanket as he shot bolt upright with both fists clenched, ready for battle. With recognition established, I advised him of his elevation in the system and told him to hand over the platoon to Sgt Svenson and move into my tent. His request to bring his batman was granted.

When his side of the tent was indicated, he and the batman became busy little beavers levelling a piece of ground and covering it with grass and heather to make a soft under-layer for the bedding. Reg then stretched out on it and, with a luxurious yawn, declared, "This is what I've always wanted: a bludger's life!"

I was not impressed with this attitude and decided to establish a working arrangement early in the piece.

"Are you sure you are quite comfortable?"

"You bet."

"Bed all right?"

"Beaut."

"Well, your first job is to go down the hill and locate our F Echelon vehicles. Supervise the unloading of the trailers and send any kits of the dead or wounded to B Echelon. Check that all platoons have a complete supply of reserve ammunition. Ensure that vehicles have a top-up of petrol and have been serviced. Then report back to me."

Reg looked a bit confused.

"You don't mean right away, Boss?"

"I most certainly do mean right away."

Reg remained my 2iC until I was wounded in the attack on Chisan, in March 1951. We worked well together and became firm friends, and I never regretted the arrangement.

Shortly after Lt Angus McDonald joined the company and took command of 1 Platoon. I do not think Angus hailed directly from the land of the bagpipes and heather, although he had certain Scottish characteristics: dour, introspective, not easy to get alongside. Nevertheless, he came to us with first-class credentials, having been a commando in New Guinea during World War II. He quickly settled in and proved to be a fine platoon commander.

At this stage our only deficiency was an officer for 2 Platoon, but I was not really concerned about this. Sgt Harris seemed to have the platoon under control and I had no reason to believe they would not perform satisfactorily for him. As far as could be ascertained, A

Company was now ready to test its strength on something worthy. Preferably not too worthy at first.

FIVE

RUNNING AWAY

The UN Army commenced its intrepid advance towards the Chinese border in support of MacArthur's "Home by Christmas" promise, and the Commonwealth Brigade was placed in the backwater of Corps reserve. That the war was over for us was confirmed when we received operation "Defrost". Terms such as "billeted" and "bivouac" had a nice homely ring.

OPERATION DEFROST

Gun
1. As the result of the resumption of the gen offensive by 1 US Corps, 27 Brit Comth Bde has been placed in corps res and will be billeted in gen area Pakchon.
2. Duration of period in corps res cannot be stated, but a period of 14 days may be anticipated.

Intention
3. 3 RAR less A and B ech will bivouac gen area sq 2200.

Method
4. ... etc

On 24 November the Allied general offensive commenced and the next day we moved to "Defrost", one thousand kilometres north of Pakchon. However, MacArthur's "Home by Christmas" message did not get through to the Chinese Communist Forces (CCF). On the 25th the Chinese began their Second Phase Offensive and were attacking IX Corps in the Kunu-ri area. On the morning of the 27th the Commonwealth Brigade was ordered in support of IX Corps, and moved to harbour in a creek bed in Kunu-ri. Thus Operation Defrost ended almost before it began, and we commenced our first participation in the frustration of what the Americans so aptly described as a "bug out".

We arrived in the Kunu-ri area about midday and dismounted from our vehicles amidst utter confusion. An ROK division had collapsed and fled, exposing the flank of 2 US Division. This division had then departed the scene in great haste, creating a huge gap in the IX Corps front. The Turkish Regiment happened to be in that sector, newly arrived in the country and shaking out in preparation for being committed to the line. In this state of unpreparedness they unexpectedly came under heavy attack, and one of their battalions was surrounded and desperately fighting its way out. The Commonwealth Brigade was ordered to "stand by" to take up positions on the Corps front in support of the Turks. Higher command's lack of grasp of the situation was demonstrated by the order, counter order and disorder which persisted. With monotonous regularity orders were changed, one cancelling the other. "One hour notice to move" became "immediate notice to return north, to rejoin US 25th Division". Before this could be actioned there was another order committing the brigade to supporting the US 24 Division flank. The CO told me that the brigadier had insisted that any such action must be subject to certain simple but essential prerequisites: artillery under command, and information of location of enemy units and friendly units. Corps could not provide artillery support and had no idea of locations of either enemy or friendly units. We went back to "one hour notice". Late in the afternoon they produced a new one — "immediate notice to move south, as from daylight". This was considered to be a pretty good order, because Blind Freddy could see that command had lost its grip on the current situation.

It was our experience that there was never any difficulty providing transport to insert the brigade into some nasty situation, but when it came to extracting us for movement south, none was available. This was the situation confronting us now. Our next destination was Chasan, forty kilometres away, a move we were left to make on foot. In regard to vehicles the Australian battalion was better off than the Argylls or Middlesex, who had no vehicles other than Land Rovers. We did have GMCs and 3-ton stores-carrying vehicles at B Echelon. The CO ordered the 2iC to make a dump of all the B Echelon stores and convert the trucks to troop carriers. This permitted our Transport Officer, Paddy Outridge, to provide sufficient vehicles to move two companies plus. The men were ordered to commence marching until it became their turn for pick up. Pick up started with A and C Companies, a sound arrangement from A Company's point of view.

The Argylls started marching first, with the bagpipes wailing away with some heathen tune. Bagpipes do wonders for Jocks' morale but little for mine. The music is too thin. Give me a military band with the brass in full song all the way down from tenor trumpets to the B Flat bass. I like a lot of music, robust music. I was spoiled for bagpipes way back in my corporal days in the Middle East, when I was in charge of a section billeted in a large ten-man tent. One of the occupants was a Scot by the name of Anderson, who carried bagpipes wherever he went. He must be dead by now, but I will lay a shade of odds those pipes are clutched to him still. Anderson would make a nuisance of himself night after night, squealing away on his chanter. On a really bad night he would declare, "A'Dood, ye Irish bastard, I'll go ye a wee tune on the peeps", and with this he would breathe life into that tartan monster to produce the moaning sounds associated with tuning the drones. Drones adjusted, Jock would stamp his foot and set off marching up and down the tent, squeezing the poor thing's midriff to induce torturous cry at full volume. Gone was any hope of conversation, reading, playing cards or letter writing. On a good night the sound carried as far as the Officers' Mess, causing an angel of mercy to appear with an invitation from the CO for Jock to transfer his performance to the Mess. We could still hear the bagpipes, but I contend that such music improves immeasurably in proportion to the distance from the hearer. Later in the night the angel escorted Anderson back to the tent stinking of whiskey and quite incapable of further nuisance.

Over the heavily congested roads the stop–go trip to to Chasan took in the order of six hours, so B and D companies got in a lot of marching practice before pick up. However, six hours in the back of a truck in sub-zero temperatures is only marginally preferable to marching. With the Australian movement complete, Paddy Outridge then set about moving the Argylls and the Middlesex Regiment, his drivers working well into the day of the 29th.

At Chasan the brigade again came under the command of the US 1st Cavalry Division, and 30 November developed into another day of order, counter order and disorder. The US 2nd Division, having taken a pounding, withdrew in utter confusion, but the Chinese Army had blocked the road with an ambush, preventing their retreat south. The Middlesex Regiment was dispatched to break the ambush, but they discovered the enemy in far greater strength than reported, and the task was impossible. Adding to the Regiment's troubles, the American troops opened fire on them. 3 RAR was ordered to move up and assist the Middlesex but this order was cancelled before we could get into our equipment. In the early afternoon the brigade was warned to be ready for movement, either south to Sainjang or east to Sunchon, and we sat around twiddling our fingers, waiting to find out which. Eventually the instruction came to move nine kilometres south to Sainjang on the morning of 1

December, in support of the US 5 Cavalry Regiment. We had no sooner settled in at Sainjang when, to the disgust of one and all, orders came to return to Chasan and reoccupy the position we had just vacated.[1] Confusion reigned and rumours were rife.

On the 2nd, following a most uncomfortable night sleeping in the open on frozen ground, orders were issued for movement of the battalion to Yopa-ri, where we were to guard a bridge that the US Engineers were in the process of constructing over the river.

SIX

THE BRIDGE AT YOPA-RI

On 2 December the 27 British Commonwealth Brigade again came under the command of the 1st US Cavalry Division at Sainjang, about sixty kilometres north-east of the North Korean capital, Pyongyang. This division had responsibility for protecting the east flank of the retreating United Nations forces.

The Main Supply Route (MSR) by which the United Nations forces were retreating was a road leading south from Pyongyang and west of the Taedong River. (See Map 3.) The 7th Cavalry Regiment and the Argylls were located at Songchon to protect the flank of this route during the withdrawal. However, there was fear that by the time the 7th Regiment and the Argylls were withdrawn the enemy may have cut the MSR. A secondary road ran from Songchon along the east side of the Taedong River, and it was planned that this route would be adopted, should the MSR become unavailable. To provide a crossing point for the 7th Cavalry Regiment's heavy transports and accompanying tanks, the US Engineers were constructing a bridge over the Taedong River, at Yopa-ri.

On 2 December, 3 RAR was instructed to occupy the east side of the Taedong River at Yopa-ri and secure it until all withdrawing forces had passed over the newly constructed bridge. Unfortunately, before 3 RAR could reach the area, the US Engineers were attacked by the Chinese and driven off.

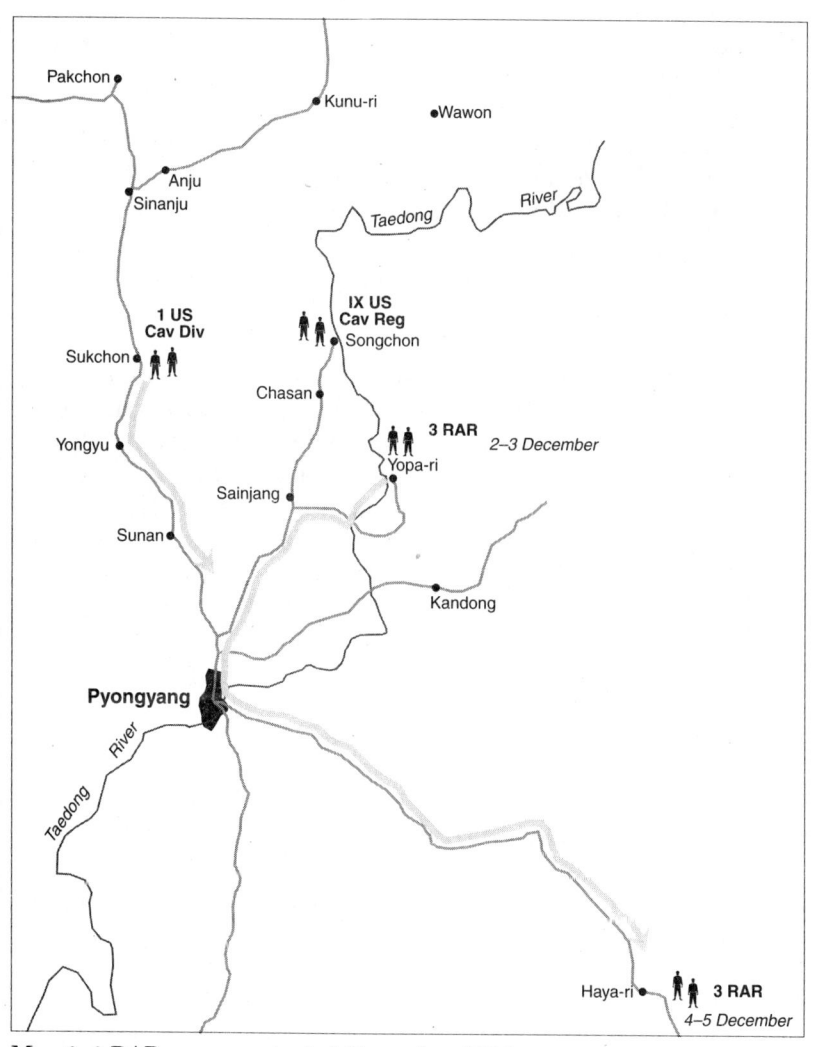

Map 3: 3 RAR movements, 2–5 December 1950

On arrival, 3 RAR moved three rifle companies across the river and into positions on the lower slopes of the feature opposite the bridge which the US engineers again had under construction. A Company occupied the north end, the direction from which the withdrawing regiments were expected. (See Map 4.)

The three rifle companies were situated at the base of a heavily wooded feature rising about 500 metres behind them. Between the river and the wooded fringe lay about 150 metres of cleared, flat ground accommodating the road. Recent heavy falls covered the ground, and everything else, with a generous blanket of fresh, crisp snow.

Without doubt the high ground above us was occupied by the enemy. This was evidenced by the treatment meted out to the US Engineers. If further confirmation was required, the Chinese blatantly advertised their presence by filling the air with an atonal concert of bugles and whistles. We were also aware that the Sunchon road we were covering was already in enemy hands. Lt John Ward's 12 Platoon, with some General Patton tanks, was dispatched on a reconnaissance patrol along the road to the north. About two kilometres from A Company they were confronted by a strong Chinese force astride the road. If the 7th Cavalry were to use that route they would most certainly have to fight their way through.

When issuing riding instructions, the CO allocated A Company a section of 17-pounder anti-tank guns. We had not seen a hostile tank since October 1950, at Chongju. The Chinese Army had come through the hills on foot and had no armour. Even if they could somehow have managed to sneak a tank into action, the Allied Air Force would have had a field day with it.

I protested that the guns had no place in my task. I had no target for such a weapon; they would be a noisy nuisance, as their GMCs would have to be started up at regular intervals to prevent cracked cylinder heads; and if we had to withdraw, after some hours set in snow they

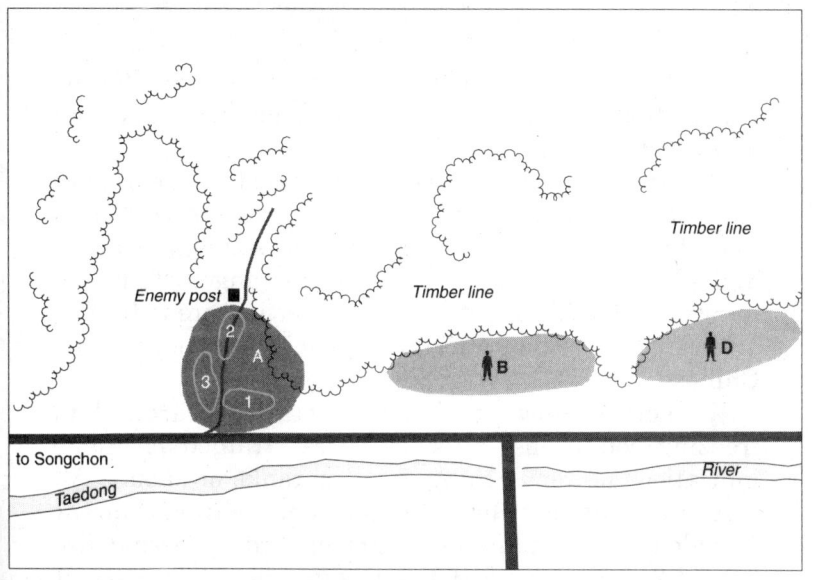

Map 4: Company positions at Yopa-ri Bridge

could be difficult to extract. In general, I made it clear that anti-tank guns were as useful to me as a sore backside was to a boundary rider. However, I was informed, in very direct language, to do as I was told.

On arrival in the designated area at about 1600 hours, I allocated the platoon positions and CSM, Tom Muggleton, laid out the headquarters. The 17-pounders were sited on the only possible approach for a tank — the direction from which we expected friendly tanks to appear.

2 Platoon was sited astride a track which led through the company perimeter and east up the hill towards the enemy. Almost immediately they got into a fight, when they surprised a Chinese outpost situated across the track. 2 Platoon launched an immediate attack and drove the enemy off. George Harris, always an aggressive platoon commander, was set to give chase and didn't take it kindly when ordered to break off and settle his troops into defence. My concern was that he could be lured into a situation requiring me to commit the remainder of the

company to extract him. As it was, there was a good chance the evicted outpost lads had gone home in a huff to get big brother.

The enemy Harris routed had established themselves in a cleared space, with cosy shelters constructed from rice stooks. Inside these shelters the soldiers' bedrolls and other possessions were carefully arranged. 2 Platoon drew considerable satisfaction from setting fire to the lot, ensuring a most uncomfortable night in the snow for the Chinese.

We settled down to hours of standing around in freezing conditions, eyes and ears strained for some indications of approaching vehicles, tanks or enemy. All was quiet except for the occasional entertainment provided by our Chinese musicians and harassing fire from 4.2 mortar and 105 mm guns, banging away at random in the high ground above us.[1]

I really irritated the Anti-Tank Section Commander by repeatedly reminding him to ensure that his guns came out clean when I ordered it. Frequently my thoughts turned to the now-completed bridge, and imagined what it would look like with companies bottle-necked during the crossing process. Our task was to hold the enemy at bay while the US Army formation passed over, but who would keep them busy while we withdrew. In the moonlight our dark uniforms stood out in the snow, inviting a slaughter if our withdrawal was opposed.

Sometime during the night the CO advised that the road we were guarding would not be used, as the Cavalry Regiment and the Argylls had withdrawn down the MSR. We were now very, very lonely, being the only UN troops east of the Taedong River and north of Yopa-ri.

Eventually approval came for A Company to commence withdrawing, with some cover provided by tanks. I had it firmly fixed in my mind that my orders were to hold until midnight, but the War Diary says 0530 hours so I must go with that.[2] There were many occasions in the Korean War when we were mystified by the enemy's contrary reaction to a simple tactical situation. It was obvious the bridge had been built to accommodate a retreating force , and the idea of wreaking havoc on the consequential defile of troops should have been too tempting for an enemy commander to pass up. The rifle companies at least should have received hostile attention as they crossed. But, even with the anti-tank tractors screaming out our intentions, we crossed the bridge to safety without incident.

With the last of 3 RAR troops clear of the bridge the Pioneer Platoon demolished it with a glorious blast of explosive. This was probably a waste of time and explosives, as the Taedong was rapidly freezing over, and soon bridges would be unnecessary.

The battalion concentrated just out of Yopa-ri, prior to movement to our next destination, Hayu-ri, some 150 kilometres away.

SEVEN

THE SLOW ROAD FROM HAYU-RI TO UIJONGBU

Early in December the tactical situation continued to deteriorate in response to the aggressive attacking of the Chinese Communist Forces. On the 4th the company commanders of 3 RAR preceded the troops on the 150-kilometre move south, to Hayu-ri. The withdrawal of the companies was conducted by 2iCs, a standard practice in those days.

On arrival at Hayu-ri the company commanders were allocated defence positions and advised that troops would be arriving later. I laid out the platoon positions and arranged guides at company HQ to conduct the troops in as they arrived. I then went to the bottom of the feature to await the arrival of the company, expecting them to be together in a complete group. The move proved to be a mess. There was no US Motor Company available for their withdrawal, so the Diggers travelled in dribs and drabs on gun limbers, tanks and all manner of vehicles in the sub-zero conditions. They were not in organised company lots but scattered throughout the mixture of vehicles. When a group arrived I would identify my frozen bunch and dispatch them up the hill to company HQ and resume my search for the remainder. It was dawn when the last of them arrived, and I made my way wearily to the shelter my staff had prepared for me. I told Reg Saunders the company was his as I was off to the sack, with a "Do Not Disturb" instruction.

I was no sooner clasped in the merciful arms of Morpheus when a severe shaking by Saunders brought the unwelcome news that the company was on "immediate stand by" for an operation and I was to report to HQ for briefing. I arrived at Battalion HQ very conscious of my unshaven condition and met the Brigade Major. He informed me that an American outfit had been ambushed somewhere on the road to the north of us. We were tasked to break through to relieve them, and a US Motor Platoon was standing by to transport us. I again marvelled at the ease with which such vehicles could be produced when we were required to go *towards* the enemy.

Having no knowledge of the location of the ambush we moved with great care, hoping to rely on the sound of firing or the presence of retreating US soldiers to home us in. We got neither. Eventually we pulled up at a point where high ground on the right of the road offered ideal ambush conditions. The company dismounted and I took two platoons up the feature, working it over from a flank. Arriving at the highest point two things became clear. The enemy, having done what it came to do, had fled the scene, and so had the Americans. The road for a thousand metres or so was littered with US Army clothing and equipment, scattered wildly about where the Chinese had ripped their way through it in search of hand-portable plunder.

It was then the Diggers turn to sift carefully through what remained of the US Army's offering, mainly searching for sleeping bags and warm items of clothing. Roy Nunan found a Catholic Missal in mint condition, no doubt the property of a US Army Chaplain. This he parcelled up and sent back to his mother. The battalion transport platoon also acquired two jeeps, unwittingly donated by the US Army.

The next day, the 6th, orders were out for another

move, this time to Singye-ni, twenty-five kilometres away, again under command of the Cavalry Division. For this move there was, of course, insufficient transport for the battalion to be moved as a whole. A and D companies drew the short straw and marched fourteen kilometres of it.

On the 8th the brigade moved further south to Sibyon-ni arriving at 0800 hours. Two hours later A Company was ordered on patrol twenty-five kilometres north to Ichon (not to be confused with another Ichon south of Seoul) to ascertain if the enemy had advanced that far. Mounted on GMCs and with a platoon of tanks and a platoon of 4.2 heavy mortars, we set off, the tanks leading and the Diggers ready to dismount and take whatever action was necessary, depending on the nature of first contact. The 4.2s brought up in the rear, to give fire support if required.

Eight kilometres down the track the road had been so efficiently demolished by US Army Engineers that it was completely impassable to vehicles, including our tanks. On reporting the situation to the CO, his instruction was to leave the transport and tanks at that location and continue the patrol on foot. We were to go as far as was possible in order to be able to return to the vehicles in daylight.

About two kilometres further on, the road ran between a river and a precipitous cliff face, the bottom of which had been shaved out to accommodate the road. I hated every moment of this patrol. If we encountered enemy tactically sited on the opposite bank of the river we would be sitting ducks, pinned against the cliff wall with nowhere to hide. If the enemy got on top of us the predicament would be no better. The best I could do was to keep the column spaced out as long as practicable, in the hope that a contact would involve as few of us as possible. This situation seemed interminable, the stuff stomach ulcers are made of, and I kept the pace down so we would traverse the minimum distance before the point of return was reached. The return journey was no more enjoyable than the outward trip, but the patrol got back without incident.

The following day, 9 December, the battalion less B and D companies moved to Kumchon nine kilometres south. Here we relieved I Company of the 187 Airborne Regimental Combat Team, which was guarding a mountain pass. This was supposed to be the heart of guerrilla territory but we had no contacts. B and D companies were detailed for protecting a radio unit, and road patrolling throughout the area.

It was at this time that we had a welcome addition to the company — Lt John Church, who took command of 2 Platoon. Church and I were well known to each other, having served together during the Occupation of Japan. John was a graduate of the Royal Military College, Duntroon. For the first time I had a full compliment of officers.

The ROK Army had a simple recruiting system. A team of armed Military Police would arrive at a village and line up all males for inspection. Those between fifteen and sixty would be taken to a manpower holding unit. From this organisation the young and fit went to the army, the others to labour units as porters or for general duties. Accounting for these conscripts was apparently non-existent. A member of our unit went to one of these camps with authority to pick up 3 RAR's allocation of porters. The person in charge just counted off the numbers required like so many sheep, and handed them over without bothering to record their names or any other detail.

The Diggers were a gregarious bunch, striking up friendships easily with Korean civilians encountered while passing through towns and villages. The language barrier was difficult to handle with the adults, but ration-pack sweets quickly overcame that problem with the children. Most companies had a couple of Korean lads adopted by the cooks. These lads were happy to work for three meals a day and a hiding place from the Korean recruiting squads. Of course they did not bear arms or go forward of B Echelon.

Our RMO, Don Beard, had a North Korean lad by the name of Yung Kim Choy working in the Regimental Aid Post. Doc sometimes facetiously referred to him as a medical orderly, but he was a general duties man. Kim Choy stayed with 3 RAR for the entire war. Eventually he emigrated to Australia and now resides in Sydney, as proudly Australian as any of us. A veteran of the Kapyong battle, he can be found at every Kapyong Day Ceremonial Parade celebration at 3 RAR.

Somewhere along the line a couple of Korean lads attached themselves to our kitchen where they laboured willingly at pot walloping and general duties. The only remuneration they expected was food and shelter, which is all they would have received in their own army. This they got with companionship thrown in, for they soon became an integral part of our team. I do not know exactly where or when we acquired them, North or South Korea, but they were with us for so long that they became as much part of the company as anyone else. One day there were angry noises emanating from the normally quiet cooks area, and I noticed some ROK soldiers there. On inquiry I was advised that there was a minor problem being attended to, and it would be a good idea if I kept out of it. This was a clear indicator that whatever was going on might not be strictly in accordance with the Army Manual of Regulations and Orders.

Somehow a recruiting squad had got wind of our boys and had come to take them away. Our gallant cooks, each ramming a round into the breech of his rifle, confronted them. They declared that the lads were executing their war service as part of the Australian Army and that there would be blood on the ground if any attempt were made to remove them. The threat worked, and the recruiting team backed off reluctantly but without further argument. This was probably for the best. Had it come to a showdown, I have serious doubts about the firing condition of the cooks' rifles, and even more about their ability to engage in a close-quarters fire fight.

EIGHT

ACTIVITIES AT UIJONGBU

On 11 December the battalion was transported 138 kilometres south to Uijongbu, a village about twenty kilometres north of Seoul. The forward troops were some eight kilometres further north, where the 6th ROK Division was holding the line. At Uijongbu the British Commonwealth Brigade was to come under IX Corps, as corps reserve.

The trip must have been murder for the soldiers huddled in open vehicles, and it was by no means comfortable for the company commanders travelling in open jeeps. Deep snow everywhere and the temperatures way below freezing made life unbearable, and the Diggers huddled and shivered, seeking refuge from the biting wind. The situation was exacerbated by the snail's pace crawl on overcrowded roads. Our convoy was motionless for hours while road priority was allocated to other formations. When movement resumed, vehicles idled along at walking pace. During one protracted stop there was a large deserted wooden building on the other side of the road where our soldiers exercised their numb legs on the lee side, sheltering from the freezing wind. Someone set the building on fire, and, as Nunan had been with the group, I accused him of arson, but with hurt indignation he denied any responsibility. I do not normally approve of wanton destruction of property, but I joined the group toasting themselves in the intense heat, turning around and around, cooking on all sides. Absolute luxury.

In this snow-decked winter wonderland 3 RAR spent the best part of three weeks in comparative peace, disturbed only by the eternal necessity of patrolling. Battalion Headquarters and Support Company attended to the niceties of soldiering by a flagpole and stone paths and other indicators of gracious living, including, according to our Signal Sergeant, Jack Gallaway, generous supplies of rum. An Officers Mess was established for the HQ staff and Support Company officers. The CO had one of the Anti-Tank Platoon's tractors, a ten-wheel GMC, converted into a caravan for his residence and office. By infantry battalion standards it was a magnificent affair: petrol heating, electric lighting, a bunk, a table with tablecloth, crockery and cutlery, radio and telephone communications and a stair to the door. There was even a high-powered Zenith radio receiver for light entertainment and to check on world affairs. This contraption was aptly designated by the Diggers as "Pandora's Box".

Meanwhile, back in the rifle companies, the platoons settled down in their allotted defence areas, pushing the snow aside where weapon pits would be if ever the occupiers could smash their way into the frozen ground. In these miserable conditions they lay their sleeping gear on the below-zero ground and tried to generate sufficient warmth for sleep. When their turn came to man the sentry's weapon pit they would be dragged from the sleeping bag to shiver out the hour or so of this duty. At the conclusion of their shift the Diggers were frozen stiff, and gratefully climbed back into their sleeping bags to thaw out again. It was no wonder we were taking more casualties from frostbite and associated cold-weather illnesses than we were from bullets.

The days were taken up with the routine duties of patrolling, manning listening posts, checking weapons etc. To pass time, any man with a deck of cards would never be short of mates. A steady beer ration helped morale, but rum or the like was not tolerated in rifle company defence areas. Rifle company officers received a share of the spirits allocated for the Officers' Mess, but I purchased all A Company allocation and stored it in my trailer, to be produced only when the operational situation was all clear.

In this location Reg Saunders and I were comfortably situated in a deserted two-room Korean mud hut which doubled as the Orderly Room and our sleeping quarters, with the headquarters personnel located around it. Korean huts had a simple but effective form of floor heating — by a duct directing smoke and heat from the cooking area fire under the floor of the hut and away through a chimney on the other side.

Of the brigade's many deficiencies, the most serious was a lack of artillery support. To assist in this regard a US Chemical Warfare battalion of 4.2 inch mortars was attached to the brigade, to fire high explosive or smoke for us. They were welcome, but they did not have the range of field artillery. Also in theatre was a US Range Finding and Flash Spotting Battalion, now surplus to requirement because the Chinese had no artillery to spot. The US Command withdrew the boffin equipment and issued 105 mm guns, ordering the Range Firing Battalion to go away and find out how to fire them. With their gunner education complete they were attached to the Commonwealth Brigade. To gain our confidence a demonstration shoot was arranged, where company commanders nominated targets for them to range in on. This was a big mistake, for their shooting was atrocious. In Nunan's considered opinion, "They couldn't hit a cow in the arse with a shovel full of wheat". Not quite how I would have put it, but it summed up the situation fairly well.

They were sent away to continue training.

Frequently company commanders were summoned to Brigade HQ for orders or general briefing on some subject or other, a session irreverently referred to as "prayers". For this I would set off with Nunan to arrive in time to check in with Lt Alf Argent's Intelligence Section, to bring my map up-to-date and catch up on the current situation in our general area. On the way back my mind would be occupied with details for briefing platoon commanders, particularly if there was a patrol task to allocate. Invariably my thoughts would be punctuated by some monologue from Nunan. On one occasion he complained of having trouble with his ears, and asked if it was alright to visit the RMO while I was at prayers. Picking him up for the return trip I inquired if he had had treatment. He said the RMO put something in his ears and gave him pills to take. As we walked a little further along the track:

"Doc says I've got Otitis Media."

"I see."

About fifteen paces further:

"You don't know what Otitis Media is, do you?"

"No Roy. Beyond that it is something to do with the middle ear."

Another fifteen paces.

"It means I've got tinea of the bloody lug."

Thinking on this I decided Roy's statement of the condition provided a better description of the ailment than the doctor's curt Latin.

During this period the company was tasked for two deep patrols. The first was a one-day affair, motoring to Pupyong-ni. This was pretty much routine and we did not expect any excitement and did not get any, except difficulty with control of the jeeps on the icy roads. Smiffy seemed to handle this by under-powering, persisting with top gear as long as possible to reduce the possibility of spinning the wheels. It was not unusual in those days to see a jeep off the road on its back, wheels in the air and motor racing, a situation Smiffy described in his delicate way as "Guts up and screaming".

The second patrol on 18 December was a different

matter. It involved approaching to a start point, an overnight bivouac in the snow, and the following day a patrol to Hyon-ni to investigate reported enemy dispositions there. To do the job I had under command a company of US 105 mm guns, a platoon of 4.2 inch heavy mortars and an Air Contact Team to call in aircraft support if necessary.

Arriving at the bivouac area we deployed tactically, banked up snow to make wind brakes and settled down to an evening meal of frozen C rations and a most uncomfortable, freezing night.

Next day our convoy approached to the mouth of the wide, long valley which lead to Hyon-ni. Here I found the headquarters of an ROK regiment set up and in business. This was not in my brief so I sought out the US KMAG officer attached as military adviser to the ROK Commander.[1] It was obvious he had not expected us and was surprised when I explained my mission, vigorously assuring me we need proceed no further, as there were no enemy in Hyon-ni. Although there were no ROK troops deployed in the valley, they had had patrols the length of it. I told him this was very reassuring but I had to check out the village. The discussion which followed got a bit confused, and it became necessary to affirm that I did not doubt his veracity, but our system of operating demanded I not return without actually putting foot in the village, personally. His answer to this was for me to leave my entourage where it was and follow him up the valley in my jeep.

I had the gunners deploy, ready to respond if I called for fire, and ordered Harold Mulry to start 3 Platoon marching up the valley behind me, in case we ran into trouble. I never had much faith in ROK information and considered it a stupid risk to do this thing unaccompanied when I had a hundred men and plenty of fire support. Nevertheless, I was in the US KMAG's territory, and in no position to argue. I had to wear it with bad grace, and took it out on Nunan:

"Nunan, your gun is pointing at Smiffy's back."

"Sorry Boss."

"Point the damned thing over the side of the jeep, where you are supposed to be searching."

"Yes Boss."

"And put a bloody magazine on it."

"Smiffy, Boss got out of the wrong side of the bed this mornin'."

I enjoyed the trip even less when we arrived at our destination. There is always an eerie atmosphere associated with a silent, deserted village. It's where one could easily come to believe in ghosts. The only discernible sign of life was an ugly individual emerging from one of the houses. The KMAG officer interrogated him in Korean and appeared to be happy with the responses. But I did not like him. Villages were places for old men, women and children. This fellow was of the age that all fun-loving Korean men were recruited for a life of adventure in their army. I had a feeling he belonged to the opposition.

However, nothing happened and the return journey was uneventful.

Later in December Brig Coad put a stop to all deep patrolling due to the number of ROK troops in the area and the possibility of an accidental fire fight developing.

That month the Commander of Eighth Army, Gen Walthem H. Walker, was killed in a jeep accident on his way to present the 27 British Commonwealth Brigade with a Korean Presidential Citation. His replacement was Matthew B. Ridgway who was given command of all forces in Korea. A unified command was a distinct change in policy. Previously command in Korea had been split. X Corps on the east coast was commanded by Gen Almond who reported directly to MacArthur in Tokyo. Walker's command included only troops in the centre and west of Korea, and he, too, reported direct to Tokyo. There had been no coordinating headquarters in Korea. The other anomaly was that Gen Almond had the duel role of command of X Corps and Chief of Staff to MacArthur.

From the beginning Ridgway declared a policy of no more retreats, rather, we would stand and fight. This sounded like a good idea, but it did not take into consideration the ROK divisions dislike of excitement, taking to the road in disorganised panic at the first Chinese battle cry.

I had an excellent soldier, Charlie Donovan, a rough-nut section commander in 1 Platoon. He had been with the platoon from the very beginning and taken part in every action involving A Company, being wounded twice, once remaining on duty. I couldn't see him impressing greatly at ceremonial soldiering but he was in his element in the situations Korea threw up. At various times corporal or private, it did not matter which, for Charlie was the natural leader of this section regardless of rank. However, our Donovan had a down side. Whenever we were in reserve he got bored and if we were in the vicinity of a city or sizable town he went missing. Unfortunately Uijongbu was quite close to Seoul and inevitably one morning CSM Muggleton reported Donovan adrift again. I decided that his platoon could take responsibility for him. With Christmas approaching, the troops were on a ration of a bottle of beer per day, and I announced that I was stopping 1 Platoon's beer ration for the period of Charlie's absence. It worked. The next day an NCO requested a loan of a jeep for a few hours to bring Donovan back. I acceded to the request without inquiring too deeply into detail I did not want to know about anyway. The jeep returned with my wandering boy and a trailer load of beer to boot. A rather good result all round. That was the last time Charlie went adrift. Years later I got a line on Donovan in Queensland, and hoped to make contact with his colourful character on a trip I had scheduled there. Sadly Charlie did not wait for me. He had gone adrift again, and this time to where I couldn't send a jeep to bring him back.

During December amenities began to appear in the form of parcels from friends, relatives and philanthropic organisations — the RSL, Red Cross etc. In the bleak, uncomfortable conditions of the soldiers' daily routine the improved beer ration did much to boost morale. Enjoyment of a bottle of beer was never an immediate pleasure, due to its frozen condition. The soldiers developed a variety of methods of thawing it. For me it was a matter of cuddling my Fosters overnight in my sleeping bag. A warm beer went well at breakfast, washing down my preferred combat ration of Ham and Lima Beans. We also had trouble with the combat ration main meals, which froze in the tin. For heating food or making a brew we were issued with a small amount of solid fuel, the stuff mountaineers use. To conserve the fuel a form of pressure cooking was employed. We would make a dent in the lid of the tin with the butt of the bayonet before heating. When the pressure inside the tin was sufficient to blow out the dent the contents were ready to eat. Care had to be taken in opening the tin, however, for a jet of boiling gravy had to be anticipated.

Christmas Eve I retired early. There was something on in the headquarters mess but, for whatever reason, I did not attend it. At some time during the night I awoke to find Smiffy and Nunan alongside my bunk proffering a bottle of Korean moonshine, which they claimed to be the answer to a connoisseur's prayer. It was obvious they had been on the local booze. Nunan was talking in shorthand and Smiffy had a precarious sway. The label on the bottle declared it to be Wah Rang Brandy and portrayed a ferocious, sword-wielding Genghis Kahn. Under him was the assurance: "Very old. Specially selected for the American Forces."

The CO had just published a Routine Order declaring the consumption of local brews a hanging offence. I was quick to remind the pair of this and they responded by shoving the foul-smelling concoction under my nose, pleading that they had obtained it at great trouble and shocking expense, with the sole intention of having a Christmas drink with me. Touching ! To prove it was not lethal Smiffy took a good swig, then, always a stickler for etiquette, wiped the neck of the bottle on his tunic before handing it to me. Long ago I had learned that "If you can't beat 'em, join 'em". I took a swig and shuddered as the foul brew hit my stomach. I wished them a happy and holy Christmas, and ordered them to bed before I sent for CSM Muggleton.

As December drew to a close we had evidence that the enemy was on the move again, when refugees began fleeing before the approaching Chinese Army. We never became hardened to the sight of these unfortunate victims of war: women, old men and children, plodding along, exposed to the punishing Korean winter, their meagre possessions on their backs or in push carts, barrows and the like. Where they would spend the night didn't bear thinking about. Towards the end of the month the volume of refugees increased to flood proportions, making it obvious that the opposition was about to erupt on to the scene again.

It was while the brigade was in Uijongbu that the seven days Rest and Recreation Leave (R & R) to Japan was introduced for personnel who had been in the Korean theatre for a prescribed period. One of the A Company R & R groups consisted of a team of men well capable of handling themselves in a tight corner. Heading this team was Sgt George Harris, a one-time prelim boy at Melbourne Stadium, and with him were other big men equally capable of acquitting themselves effectively in any situation. Individually they were formidable, collectively a disaster. On return from R & R Sgt Harris reported to me:

"Skipper. We are in big trouble."

"I don't think I want to hear about this George."

"Oh. You're going to hear about it alright, when the charge reports get here."

According to George they had arrived in Tokyo in good shape and set out to investigate the delights the city offered to comfort the battle-weary soldier. They entered the Ginza Beer Hall, sat at a table with two GIs, also battle weary, and ordered a beer all round. One of the Americans had obviously consumed far more than his fair share of booze and had reached a playful mood. As a mini-skirted Japanese waitress went by he would give her an affectionate pat on the rear end. There were five American Military Police at the door and one of them approached the table and thumped it with his night stick, warning against any future affectionate patting. The Yank was past benefiting from warnings and soon repeated the offence, whereupon the MP strode across the room and flattened him with a whack across the back of his neck, laying him out face down on the table. It was the unnecessary violence of this assault which upset the group. As George put it:

"He was a big stand over bastard, Boss and you would have had a go too, if you'd been there."

"I don't think so, George."

The outcome was that one of our group flattened the MP. This called for the remaining law enforcers to get involved, and a general free-for-all ensued.

"We didn't let A Company down, Boss," said George. "We got stuck in and gave a good account of ourselves."

Obviously I was expected to feel great pride in all this. Inevitably the riot squad burst on the scene and the bunch were accommodated in the cage at US Army Military Police Headquarters. A Red Cap with a 15 cwt van took responsibility for them, handing them over to the Australian Military Depot at Ebisu.

For them to appear in Tokyo again would invite severe retribution from the American MPs, and to avoid this they were transferred to an Australian leave hotel at Kawana. Here they had an unexpected reunion with some other A Company warriors on convalescence from wounds received earlier. A convivial time followed sampling a variety of drinks during the afternoon. Following dinner they attended the night's entertainment, a concert of some sort. At this stage one of them was overcome by all the activities, and fell quietly asleep. With the close of proceedings all except sleeping beauty stood for the National Anthem. This upset an officer, who made the fatal mistake of grasping the sleeper by the shirt front, ordering him to stand up for the King. The offender came out of his sleep and, in a confused reflex action, flattened the cause of his aggravation. Next day the group were put on a train back to Ebisu. Here they were held in close arrest until escorted to an aircraft and returned to Korea.

The charge sheets arrived in the closing days of December, but with a CCF offensive imminent this was no time for busting a sergeant or losing valuable fighting men, so I told the company clerk, Cpl Lennie Taylor, to bury the charge sheets in the bottom of the company box,[2] for some future action. The following months were packed with adventure and I completely forgot about the charges. They were still there five months later when I left Korea and they did not surface for a month or two after that. The disciplinary action meted out was appropriate, though not too severe.

At this stage I had commanded the company for six weeks without a major confrontation with the enemy. Things were about to change.

NINE

TOKCHONG: A PERILOUS WITHDRAWAL

There was no surprise on the 1st of January when the Chinese attacked 6 ROK Division and, true to form, the division broke and ran, leaving the flanks of neighbouring formations exposed.[1] The British Commonwealth Brigade was then committed as a blocking force, with 3 RAR as its most northerly defence, at Tokchong. The Argylls and Middlesex were disposed in rearguard positions, a few kilometres back down the road.

The entire time at Uijongbu we were on short notice to move, so there was little confusion at 0830 hours on New Year's Day 1951 when the order came to proceed to Tokchong. Mounted on US Motor Company GMCs with tanks leading the way, the battalion made good time on the short run north. Enemy contact came early during the approach, when the US tanks were instrumental in driving off an enemy post on the Tokchong road. Nevertheless, there were casualties in Support Company and Battalion Headquarters from machine-guns fired from Tokchong village.

The area A Company was to defend was on the crest of a precipitous feature overlooking a wide valley. The only approach to the company was both steep and devoid of cover, so we were confident of being able to keep an attacker very busy. The valley floor and opposite slope were teeming with Chinese soldiers, darting hither and thither like a nest of busy ants. A US 105 Artillery battalion was under command of the brigade but it had been away, shooting for the ROK Divisions. I know they returned to our area but probably too late for allocation to companies. I certainly did not have a Forward Observation Officer (FOO). No one else was banging away with ranging rounds on the targets displayed in the valley and slopes opposite.

The company had settled into the routine of digging weapon pits and general defence activity when advice was received that the enemy had broken through and was going for our flanks. The company commanders were ordered to assemble and rendezvous with the CO some eight kilometres south of the battalion. Nothing irritates the Digger more than to get himself nicely dug in and then to be ordered to move without firing a shot from his weapon pit. The instruction to withdraw drew the usual, "Why can't the bastards make up their minds?"

This withdrawal was to be conducted by company 2iCs. I handed the company over to Reg Saunders and with my orderly, Nunan, headed for my jeep down on the road. My radio operator, Lofty Heweston, had erected his long antennae which would take some time to pull down and pack up, so I told him to take our Russian jeep when he was ready and catch up with me down the road — a decision which was to save his life.

The O Group convoy had gone only a few hundred metres when progress was blocked. The enemy machine-guns were firing at a bend in the road as it took a left turn, exposing the road to firing from machine-guns located somewhere in Tokchong. They were also spraying the road we were using. A burst hit Cyril Hall's HQ Support Company jeep, wounding one of the occupants, bursting a tyre and causing the vehicle to roll into a ditch. I heard a long burst of machine-gun fire sending bullets crackling down the line in our direction. I yelled "Get down!" and at the same time gave Smiffy a big push. A bullet smacked into the back of the jeep, through the

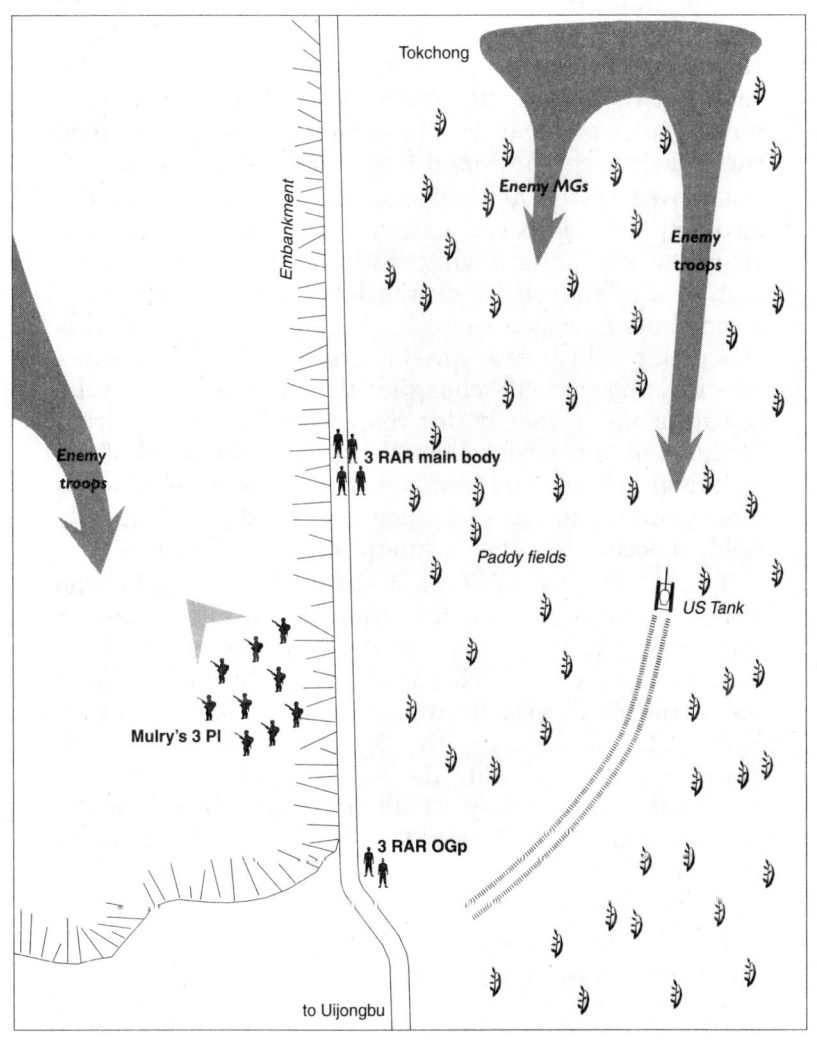

Map 5: Withdrawal from Tokchong, 1 January 1950

sleeve of Smiffy's tunic and out the metal strip below the windscreen in front of the steering wheel. Smiffy was forever grateful for that push and bored everyone in sight about the bullet holes in his jacket and the jeep. Lofty Heweston turned a pale shade of white when he later saw that the bullet had entered the jeep right where he always sat, immediately behind Smiffy. Had he not taken the Russian jeep he would have been a dead man.

I moved to the head of the column where a US 105 Artillery FOO jeep sat stationary in the middle of the road, its occupants having made a hasty departure on foot. Where the road took the left turn, a peninsula of wooded land projected into the bare paddy fields. Across this paddy field an enterprising group of Chinese soldiers was heading from Tokchong for the tip of the peninsula, to cut us off. Obviously this represented a serious threat to the road, our position on it and the withdrawal of the battalion in general. It was therefore a huge relief when a tank ran the length of the peninsula and into the paddy field, shooting the enemy group back into Tokchong.

The presence of the tank had the effect of easing the attention we were receiving from the machine-guns in Tokchong, but another threat developed immediately. A force of enemy troops began working the high ground above the road, also heading to cut us of at the bend. Most of the members of the O Group were armed with .38 revolvers, and while these had murderous effect in American movies, they would not strike fear into the hearts of our enemy. I was at a loss as to what to do to recover the situation when the welcome face of Reg Saunders appeared around the corner:

"What's the hold-up, Boss?"

"Is the company with you?"

"Yes."

"Give me a platoon."

"Which platoon do you want?"

"Any bloody platoon!"

Reg sent me 3 Platoon, commanded by the irrepressible

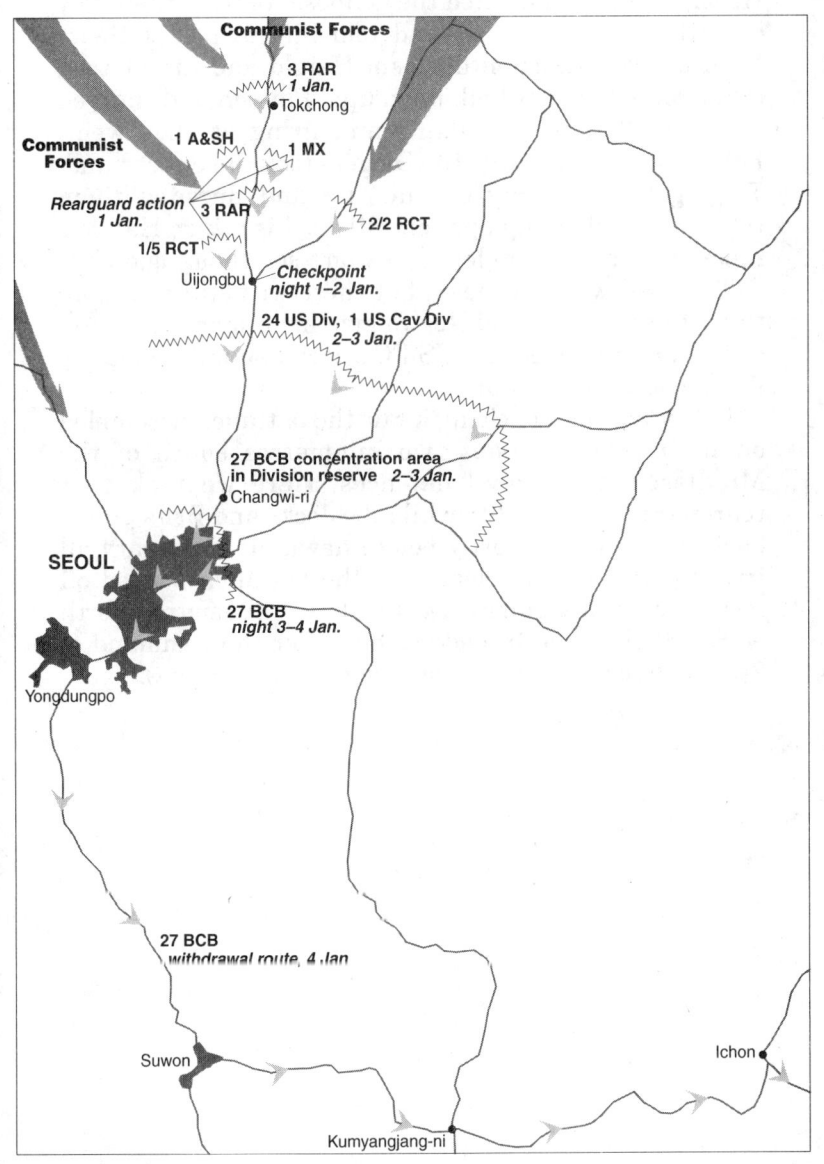

Map 6: 3 RAR movements, 1–4 January 1951

Harold Mulry. I indicated the Chinese working their way over the slope above us and told him to attack them. With characteristic enthusiasm Harold and his Platoon Sergeant, Charlie Scholl, lined up 3 Platoon and charged into the Chinese, screaming and firing as they went. Following a brief scuffle the Diggers took the upper hand. They got the enemy on the run and pursued them relentlessly, shooting up their tail. On his return Harold's report was quite simple: "You won't see them again."

The road was now open, but there was still one more thing to be done. I told Reg to give me a man who could drive, and we added the US FOO jeep to our A Company fleet. The spoils of war.

Following the Tokchong affair the battalion assembled on high ground about two kilometres south of the Middlesex and Argyll defences. Here we took over rearguard responsibility while the Jocks and Brits pulled back through us. Shortly before dawn on 2 January all friendly troops were clear, and the battalion backed off to the town of Changwi-ri, about two kilometres north of Seoul. Here the brigade came under the command of 24 US Division and became reserve for IX Corps.

TEN

ON THE RUN AGAIN

Next morning, 3 January 1951, I was instructed to take A Company to the Middlesex lines to be briefed for an important patrol operation required by 24 Division HQ. Assembled for this operation was a mixed bag of US and Commonwealth Brigade officers and a US Tank company commander. The briefing had also attracted the press. This was not a good sign — they have an infallible nose for blood.

I was informed that the forward elements of 24 Division had lost contact with the enemy and our task was to discover where they had set up business. We were to do this by the simple process of mounting A Company on tanks and charging down the Uijongbu road until we located the enemy, presumably by being fired upon. For this operation I had a company of General Patton tanks (twenty), two artillery Fire Controllers from a US 105 Artillery Battalion and an ACT with Mosquito spotter aircraft circling overhead.[1]

I found it difficult to get enthusiastic about this operation. If the enemy fired on us while we were approaching their defences, well and good; we could about turn and make for home, having achieved our aim. If, however, the Chinese let us get among them, or, worse, through them, before declaring their presence, the Diggers would be shot up from both sides. If this happened, we were supposed to dismount and engage the enemy while the tanks turned round, then remount and go for home. This sounded fine in the briefing room, but no account was taken of the fact that we might have to recover casualties and load them on to tanks under fire. General Pattons packed a lot of firepower, and no doubt would be spraying small arms and gunfire about the place. Nevertheless, the exposed infantry would still be vulnerable to fire from an enemy in dug-in defences.

I also saw that it might be difficult to get control of the situation once dismounted from this long line of tanks. In the middle of a fire fight, I would have to trust the ACT and Mosquito to identify friendly troops and locate their own targets. Registration of artillery would take time and was only applicable if the battle became a protracted affair, perish the thought! It was going to be a very messy operation.

Arriving at 24 Division forward defences, I allocated platoons to tanks and mounted up, ready for the order to go. Then came the first hitch. At the briefing I had been informed I should ride inside the command tank, so that I would be able to keep track of events throughout the column during movement. I was further told that the tanks had a separate radio system whereby I could talk with my platoon commanders. Settling myself in the command tank I requested a routine radio check with the platoon commanders. The Tankie admitted that they used to have such a facility but it was no longer operable. This was a stupid situation. There was no point in sitting inside a tank, out of communication with my platoon commanders. I opted for all officers to enjoy the exhilarating experience of clinging to the outside of a tank rattling along at speed.

We were no sooner settled down and comfortable when the order came through to dismount and "stand by". This called for more "Why can't the bastards make up their minds?" and this time I agreed with them. Up until now we had been busy getting set for whatever was going to happen. Mentally we were steeled to get on with the job. Now there was time to think and sweat, the gut turning over, the mental pictures forming of the many things that might go wrong.

After about an hour of inertia two events assisted "the bastards" to "make up their minds". First the US Air Force attacked the forward battalion of 24 Division. It was encouraging to note that they bombed their own troops as well as their allies. Then the listening posts of the forward screen withdrew in great haste to their respective battalions, with the information that the enemy was on the doorstep and probably going around the back. We generally treated US patrol reports as suspect and over-dramatised. However, these reports were sufficient for the tank-mounted operation to be aborted, and we regarded them as very good reports indeed.

But that was not the end of it! An enterprising US War Correspondent had turned in his story of the patrol in anticipation of its execution. In the *New York Post* we were credited with a dramatically successful operation, going all the way to Uijongbu. Now, that's the way to fight a war, sheath the sword and leave the fighting to journalists!

During that day, 3 January, the decision was taken to withdraw the United Nations Army about one hundred kilometres south, to defence Line D. For this operation the Commonwealth Brigade had rear-guard responsibility for holding the Seoul — Uijongbu road to cover withdrawal of the 19th and 21st US Regimental Combat Teams. The brigade was sited on a high ridge in the north of Seoul, astride the road, the Middlesex Regiment on the left and 3 RAR on the right. The Argylls were in the rear, guarding the bridge over the Han River, which had been prepared for demolition when the last troops were across.

D Company was in forward defence astride the road, with patrols forward. A Company was located on a high feature at the right rear, and was only likely to fight if things went horribly wrong.

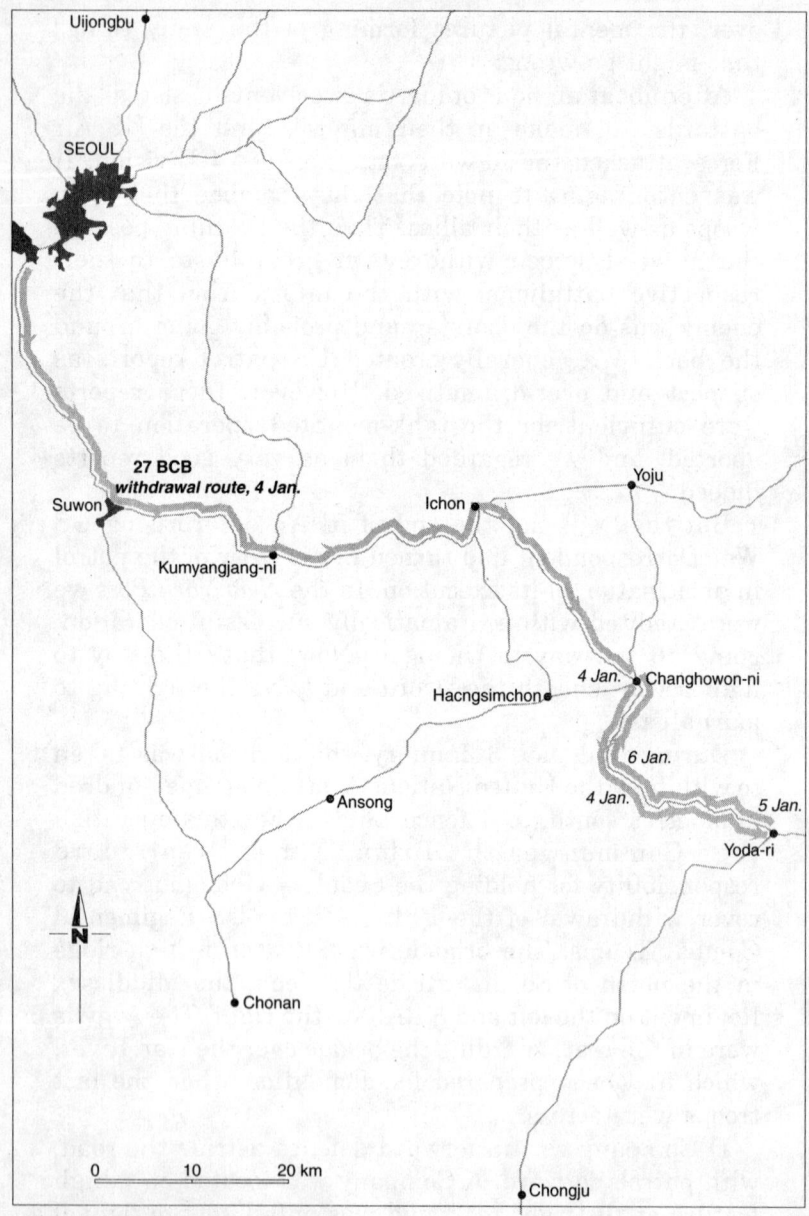

Map 7: Withdrawal to Changhowon-ni

A checkpoint had been organised to filter the flood of refugees, to give an early indication of enemy attempts to infiltrate to our rear using the refugees as cover. During the night D Company had several contacts, but in our area all was quiet. It was just a matter of sitting out the hours of another freezing Korean winter night, stamping feet and flapping arms. At 0600 hours the battalion successfully withdrew and commenced the frustrating stop–start drive on overcrowded roads to Line D.

ELEVEN

THIRTY-TWO KILOMETRES OF NO MAN'S LAND

Following the withdrawal from Seoul the battalion commenced the tedious 156-kilometre, snow-covered haul to Yoda-ri via Ichon, over the usual overcrowded roads. Again the companies were under the command of the 2iCs while the commanders proceeded independently for rendezvous with the CO at Yoda-ri. The main body of troops reckoned the war was over for them when their convoy arrived at a harbour where allied ships were loading supplies. Their hopes were soon dashed, however, when it was discovered that the leading elements had confused the sign indicating the port of "Inchon" with the town of "Ichon".

Checking in with the CO at Yoda-ri, the Orders Group party was directed to double back thirty-two kilometres north, to a defence line code-named "Line D", and a new location west of the town of Changhowon-ni. This presented a problem in that we were out of petrol, having driven the last kilometre or so on fresh air. Smiffy lined up in the queue at a US Army petrol point, where vehicles were filled from forty-four gallon drums on the back of a GMC. Smiffy and Nunan got into a slanging match with the US NCO in charge, who insisted that his orders did not include filling "furreners" vehicles. However, he relented when I explained that the petrol was to take us thirty-two kilometres north, towards the enemy, not on the bug-out route south, the general direction for US vehicles that day.

At Changhowon-ni another Orders session was conducted and company defence areas allocated. In due course our troops arrived and settled down to clearing away snow and chipping at the frozen ground in an attempt to dig weapon pits. From the battalion defences it was possible to see a good 1000 metres to the front. Deeper patrols established that there were no enemy within 7000 metres. Life in this secure situation settled into a steady, relaxed routine of improving weapon pits, manning listening posts and, of course, the eternal routine of local and deep patrolling, well forward of the battalion.

A second briefing gave us details of the next withdrawal, to Line E, ninety road kilometres further south. There was a Plan A and a Plan B for this eventuality. Plan A covered the situation of a non-contact withdrawal with movement by transport. Plan B was to be activated if a fighting withdrawal was necessary. It required companies to move twelve kilometres on foot to a designated assembly area. Reconnaissance was carried out for both plans.

Confusion and uncertainty about the direction of the war was common throughout the army. I was told of a notice someone pinned to the inside of a toilet door in Corps Headquarters, which read: "Congratulations! At this moment you are the only man in Korea who knows what he is doing."

The conduct of withdrawals and the planning of future rearward action played havoc with morale. They created a defeatist atmosphere, particularly among conscripted troops. A move south to Line E would exacerbate the problem, as it put the allies in range of the evacuation port of Pusan. Gen Ridgway was obviously concerned about the state of morale within the US Forces and published what, in our parlance, would be an "Order of the Day". It was intended for the US troops but it got general distribution:

SUBJECT: WHY WE ARE HERE

1. *In my brief period of command duty here I have heard from several sources, chiefly from the members of combat units, the questions, "Why are we here?", "What are we fighting for?"*

2. *What follows represents my answers to those questions governments. As Commander- In-Chief, United Nations Command, General of the Army Douglas MacArthur said publicly yesterday : "This command intends to maintain a military presence in Korea just so long as the Statesmen of the United States decide we should do so." The answer is simple because further comment is unnecessary. It is conclusive because the loyalty we give, and expect, precludes any questioning of these orders.*

4. *The second question is of much greater significance, and every member of this command is entitled to a full and reasoned answer. Mine follows.*

5. *To me the issues are clear. It is not a matter of this or that Korean town or village. Real estate is, here, incidental. It is not restricted to the issue of freedom for our South Korean Allies, whose fidelity and valour under the severest of stresses of battle we recognise : though that freedom is a symbol of the wider issues, and is included among them.*

6. *The real issues are whether the power of western civilisation, as God has permitted it to flower in our own beloved lands, shall defy and defeat communism : whether the rule of men who shoot their prisoners, enslave their citizens, and deride the dignity of men, shall displace the rule of those to whom the individual, and his individual rights are sacred : whether we are to survive with God's hand to guide and lead us, or to perish in the dead existence of a Godless world.*

7. *If these be true, and to me they are beyond any possibility of challenge, then this has long since ceased to be a fight for freedom for our Korean Allies alone and for their national survival. It has become, and it continues to be,*

a fight for our own freedom, for our own survival, in an honourably, independent national existence.

8. *The sacrifices we have made, and those we shall yet support, are not offered vicariously for others, but for our own direct defence.*

9. *In the final analysis, the issue now joined right here in Korea is whether communism or individual freedom shall prevail, and, make no mistake, whether the next flight of fear-driven people we have just witnessed across the Han, and continue to witness in other areas, shall be checked and defeated overseas or permitted, step by step, to close in on our own homeland and at some future time, however distant , to engulf our own loved ones in all its misery and despair.*

10. *These are the things for which we fight. Never have members of any military command had a greater challenge than we, or a finer opportunity to show ourselves and our people at their best ... and thus be an honour to the profession of arms, and a credit to those who have bred us.*

M. B. Ridgway
21 January 1951

By now our troops had been fairly well kitted out for the Korean winter conditions. Sensible water-resistant boots were provided, and we had the inner liners for the US Army jackets and sleeping bags. However, we were still losing men to frostbite, particularly in the feet, and the RMO, Doc Beard, had the challenge of coming up with a solution to the problem. During the day sweat accumulated in the socks and froze to ice when activity ceased, but for obvious reasons soldiers have to sleep with their boots on. We had been issued with at least two pairs of thick socks. Directions from Don Beard required that boots were to be removed each night, the feet massaged, and a dry pair of socks put on. The damp pair of socks was then to be worn inside the jacket to dry out for the next night. The body odour thus generated would have precluded us from dinner at Buckingham Palace, but fortunately we were all in the same condition and did not notice. Of course it was difficult to ensure that soldiers complied with those instructions and went through the correct procedures. So Doc Beard had to come up with a subtle ploy to get the message across. US Army rations provided an abundance of Barbasol shaving cream, which our soldiers would not use, favouring shaving soap, so there was always a surplus of the stuff. Doc came up with the discovery that this cream had amazing therapeutic properties. If rubbed vigorously into the feet when changing socks, or into other exposed parts, it could prevent frostbite. It was, of course, the massage, not the Barbasol, which did the job, but the deception worked. Doc Beard's Barbasol panacea became legend. The troops reckoned if they reported sick with any malady he would simply prescribe a tube of Barbasol, with instructions to rub it on the affected area.

The other other body parts most exposed to the cold were the hands. Touching metal, and all weapons are metal, resulted in skin and flesh being left behind. Exposure, of course, brought on frostbite. Need I say that Barbasol was a mighty prophylactic in this regard also. The real remedy was simple and obvious — gloves — and in due course these were issued.

Dr Don Beard had been a Major during the early days of the Korean War, a surgeon in the General Hospital in Kure. The RMO of a battalion is a Captain, so the rank of Major made him secure from the discomfort of active service with us. However, early in 1951 we again found ourselves minus an RMO, and Don busted himself back to Captain to tend to the medical needs of our soldiers. This responsibility fell to him at a period when we were loosing more men from frostbite than any other cause, the problem being exacerbated by the mobile state of 3 RAR's operations in that period. I have no doubt there were times when he regretted this unselfish move, but the Diggers never did.

While in this location the companies were equipped with a new company net radio, the 88 set. This was a revolution in communications between Company HQ and platoons. The old walkie-talkie was effective but cumbersome and it had only one fixed frequency. The 88 set come in two pouches worn on the equipment of our operator, Ossie Osbaldiston. One pouch contained the radio and the other the battery. It had multiple frequencies with switch access, providing the capacity to contact platoons of other companies if necessary. From this time there were never any communication problems between my headquarters and the platoons.

It is Standing Operating Procedure in defence that company commanders are responsible for liaison with the sub-unit on their right. On our right lay a large gap between us and the Argylls, and I instituted section-strength clearing patrols to them, morning and evening. I took Reg Saunders with me for an initial liaison visit to the Argyll company commander. There was the usual friendly greeting with a hospitable brew of tea. As we were making our farewells the company commander drew me aside to ask why I had an American 2iC. This threw me, until I realised that Reg Saunder's colour plus his American jacket and pile cap had caused the confusion. The Jock officer expected all the black officers in Korea to be Afro–Americans. For my part, I had been in continuous close contact with Reg since early November, and had completely forgotten that there was anything unusual about his appearance.[1]

During our time at Changhowon-ni the brigade got a great boost in morale with the arrival of the 16th New Zealand Field Regiment and their 25-pounder guns. Here was an artillery unit from our part of the world, with compatible operating procedures and firing the gun we had been brought up on. It was a big day when Capt Harry Honnor joined us as the A Company NZ Artillery Forward Observation Officer.

One day Lt John Church came to me with a situation which had arisen between him and his Platoon Sergeant, George Harris. He complained of Harris being uncooperative and rude. This gave me a problem because

Harris had served the company well, as Platoon Sergeant and Platoon Commander. Had Church laid formal charges I would have had no option but to refer the matter to the CO, for disciplinary action. In the circumstances, sorting out the problem was my responsibility. I could have effected a reshuffle of the platoon sergeants, but Vic Svenson was well dug in at 1 Platoon with Angus McDonald, and Harold Mulry and Charlie Scholl were inseparable in 3 Platoon. I decided on a cooling-off period. There had been complaints from the Diggers that other companies had better amenities coming forward than we were getting. I removed a very reluctant Harris from his platoon and sent him to B Echelon to investigate the situation — to find out what was available generally and if we were getting our fair share of it. Harris's stint at B Echelon did lead to an improvement in amenities. However, I could not retain him there for ever, and it was fortuitous that Vic Svenson was hospitalised with something or other. Harris filled in as platoon sergeant of 1 Platoon and Cpl Jack Sheppard MM took over as temporary platoon sergeant of 2 Platoon. Eventually, when Svenson returned, I had to put Harris back with John Church, hoping that absence had made the hearts grow a little fonder. It probably hadn't, but a position did not arise where drastic action was required. Later, when Church was wounded at Chisan, Harris again took over command of this platoon, remaining in that position until 22 April when Lt Lou Brumfield joined us at Kapyong.

Eventually it was established that the nearest enemy was about thirty-two kilometres away, just north of the town of Ichon. It was clear that the UN Command had continued to withdraw long after the enemy had given up the chase. To keep an eye on Chinese activities in the Ichon area, a platoon-strength patrol was positioned there — one day Australian and the next American. On 16 January John Church was tasked to take 2 Platoon to Ichon and remain there until first light on the 17th.[2]

A radio relay station was situated with the patrol and operated successfully during daylight, but, consistent with the equipment we had in those days, it faded out after dark.

Church positioned an outpost section, commanded by Cpl Everleigh, some 400 metres forward of the platoon. During the night this patrol observed forty to fifty enemy approaching in single file from the north. Everleigh laid ambush and ordered that no man was to fire until he gave the lead by opening up first. Discipline was good, with everyone staying low in the snow as the Chinese unwittingly walked into the trap. Everleigh allowed the enemy to advance until the head of their column was just passing through the ambush. He then took aim and got the first man, and the rest of the section let fly with Bren machine-guns, Owen guns, rifles and 36 grenades. Although the surprise was complete, the enemy backed off and engaged the section with machine-gun and rifle fire before withdrawing. Twenty of the enemy were killed in this short, well-conducted action by Everleigh's section.[3]

Everleigh returned his section to 2 Platoon and Church began withdrawing back to battalion. He dispatched his jeep to arrange for transport to meet them somewhere along the track. Unfortunately the jeep overturned on the icy road a few kilometres short of battalion, requiring the driver to walk the remainder of the distance. The delay resulted in 2 Platoon marching the best part of the way home, in the freezing pre-dawn conditions.

It was decided that future Ichon patrols would be company strength. Capt John Callander took B Company on the next patrol and spent the period pretty much without incident.

TWELVE

PATROL TO ICHON

I withdrew the company leaving an officer and four fine men behind, and they became prisoners of the enemy. Any commander who puts his troops in a position where they are taken prisoner has a bad time with his conscience, but agonising over it then and since, I do not see I had a viable option.

The War Diary of 3 RAR records that between 14 and 19 January six patrols had spent the night at Ichon, three from 3 RAR and three from US 5 Infantry Regiment. A Company was tasked for the seventh patrol, on 20 January, to take over from US F Company, 5 Infantry Regiment.

The site of the Ichon Patrol Base was twenty-nine kilometres north of the battalion — a great expanse of no man's land by any standards. A communications relay station with telephone and radio was set up about eight kilometres to the rear of the company base. This was under the control of a Signal Platoon Corporal, Stewart (Stewey) Duncan. The station was situated west of the road, beside a stream over which a narrow bridge had been constructed. Here a small detachment from B Company, commanded by Cpl Clem Kealy, was left to protect the relay station.

A deep blanket of crisp snow covered the ground and the air was still and cloudless, promising a freezing night. There was excellent visibility from a bright, full moon, the typical setting for Chinese night operations. Reports

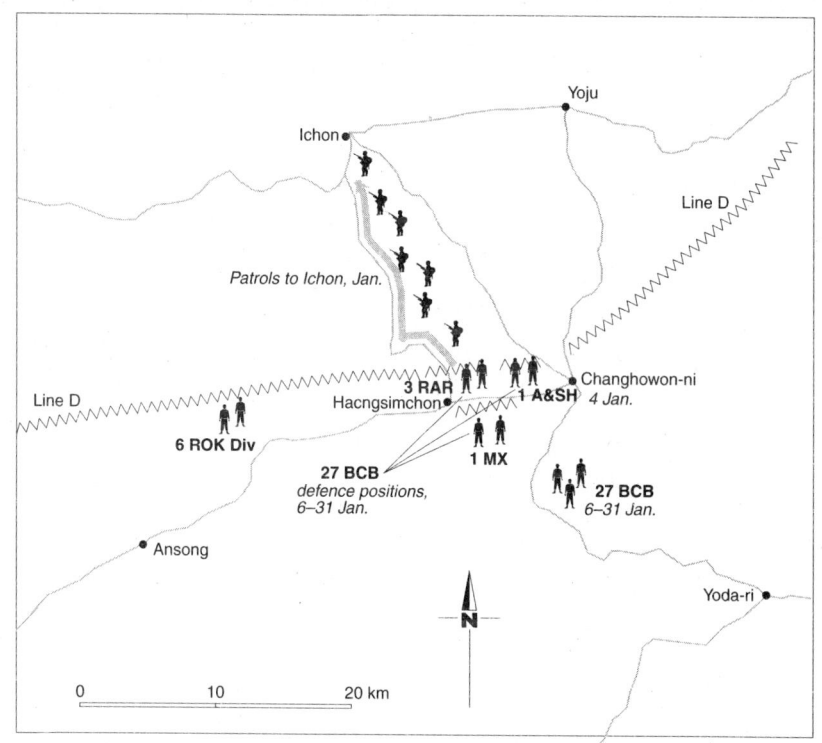

Map 8: Patrols to Ichon

from local civilian sources informed us that the enemy had laid telephone lines into the area. Not good news.

Arriving at Ichon I contacted the commander of F Company, but he could not provide any more information than I already had. Guides led my platoons to the F Company platoon positions for relief in the line. This complete, the Americans departed with handshakes and "Good luck, Aussie". I moved my headquarters astride the road, between the two forward platoons, at a cutting overlooking the steep, wide valley and the forward slopes of the high feature opposite. 1 Platoon commanded by Lt Angus McDonald was on the left, 2 Platoon under Lt John Church on the right, with a listening post forward down the track. The listening post was commanded by Cpl Jim Everleigh and positioned to give warning of enemy approach. Lt Harold Mulry's 3 Platoon was separate from the main body, guarding a road leading in from the north-east.

In a briefing by the CO as we were departing he instructed me to use a patrol to establish whether the enemy had defences on the forward slopes of the feature on the opposite side of the valley.[1] This mission I gave to Angus McDonald, a quiet but very experienced officer.

I visualised this patrol to be of sufficient strength to fight if necessary, but just before nightfall Angus approached me with the proposition that he could do the task with a small, easier to manage reconnaissance group. He told me he had four ex-commandos in his platoon who were versed in this sort of thing. The proposal made sense and since McDonald was confident of tackling the problem in this way I acceded to his request.

My instructions to McDonald included:

- To search for signs of enemy occupation on the lower slopes of the feature which our patrol occupied.
- If no contact was made, to proceed across the valley and up the feature opposite as far as time would permit, to establish if the enemy had defences there.
- To return to the company position by first light.
- In the event that our company came under attack while the patrol was out he was not to attempt to come in behind it, but to side-slip to the east and make his own way back to battalion lines.

Shortly after dark, about 1815 hours, McDonald's patrol got under way (with Cpls Buckland and Buck and Ptes Light and Hollis) and we settled down to sit out the bitter cold of a Korean winter's night.

At some stage my attention was drawn to a procession of tiny dots in the snow way out to the west and moving in a southerly direction. I observed them for some time, as they moved very slowly and were well dispersed. We estimated they were about company strength. The question of course was "what were their intentions?" Certainly it was not just a moonlight stroll. The Chinese had observed six of our patrols operating in this area and were well aware of our strengths and dispositions. I reasoned that they were aiming to set an ambush somewhere on our route out, and there was a distinct possibility we would have to fight our way back. The logical counter move was to immediately get the company far enough back to be well south of enemy reception parties. However, we were stuck in place while McDonald's patrol was somewhere out in the valley in front of us. It was a case of sweat it out, and pray that they would return in time.

The enemy's intentions became evident when, at about 0100 hours, Cpl Everleigh's outpost was attacked by a force of Chinese approaching up the road. 6 Section fought them off with machine-guns, rifles and 36 grenades, forcing the enemy to ground, but unfortunately not before L/Cpl John Andrew was killed.[2] Everleigh then withdrew his section back to 2 Platoon. The situation was not quiet for long. Heralded by the ubiquitous bugles and whistles, the Chinese attacked on the right of the road at 2 Platoon. Church's men responded vigorously, successfully fighting off the attack. The enemy then resorted to a fire fight employing small arms, mortars and medium machine-guns which opened up from a hill out to our left, seeking us out with tracer rounds. Korea's sub-zero temperatures did not make life easy John Church wrote:

> ... we tried to bring fire down on them but the Bren gunners had trouble in getting their light machine-guns to fire because of ice which had formed in them. Foolishly one of the gunners pulled his gun apart and put the head of the piston in his mouth to warm it. He only succeeded in burning his tongue on the frozen metal. In an act of desperation he finally urinated on the offending part before reassembling the weapon.[3]

I had been around long enough to recognise that we

were being given the "fix the front and go for the rear" treatment. The company was about to be caught in a trap a long way from home. Something had to be done, and soon. On a still night sound travels a great distance over snow-covered ground, and tracer rounds spraying about further advertised our predicament. I was confident that Angus and his patrol would be aware we were under attack and would not attempt to come in behind it; they would circle away to the east and head for home. I ordered a withdrawal to the radio relay detachment, hoping this would put us outside the range of a Chinese hook. From there we could watch the situation develop until dawn, then patrol forward to check out the lay of the land. The two forward platoons were ordered to pull back, with 2 Platoon as rear guard. Mulry's 3 Platoon was instructed to rendezvous at the relay station.

While the company was still in the process of withdrawing from the forward position, the relay station came under attack from a small enemy group attempting to cross the creek by a narrow bridge. Cpl Clem Kealy reported that they sighted an enemy patrol of about ten men approaching the relay station. The Chinese patrol went to ground and sent a small party forward to the bridge to test the situation. Kealy's group opened fire and the Chinese withdrew. It transpired that this was just a Chinese reconnaissance patrol, part of a much larger force.

1 and 3 Platoons arrived at the relay station at approximately 0300 hours. Looking back we heard the thump of mortar bombs and saw the tracer and small-arms fire of another attack being launched on the positions we had just vacated. This would have been further evidence for Angus that return to the original base was now impossible.

1 and 3 Platoons were deployed for protection of the relay while I put in a call to the CO. I was in the process of briefing him on the situation and our intentions to

patrol forward again at dawn, when the enemy launched another attack. It came in across the river at 1 Platoon, supported by machine-gun fire and mortars firing high-explosive bombs and illuminating flares. A confusing situation developed which wasn't easy to get a handle on. However, the Diggers poured fire into the attackers, reducing the situation to a fire fight across the moonlit creek.

2 Platoon was having a bad night. While approaching the relay station they ran into the cross-fire being exchanged between the enemy and 1 and 3 Platoons. To avoid it, John Church circled his troops east behind 3 Platoon, to pick up the road south of the battle area.

Two groups of enemy were reported, each about thirty strong, so we had the same problem again. To permit ourselves to be pinned down here would invite the Chinese to loop south again, to set up ambush somewhere along the twenty-six kilometres to the battalion. I dispatched the relay crew in their jeep then pulled out 1 and 3 Platoons and set off once more. Some distance down the road we halted at a deserted village to wait until 2 Platoon caught up. At this point I contacted the CO on the command net, reporting the situation and requesting transport. It duly arrived and the company returned to the battalion.

For the next few days we kept hoping that McDonald and his team would show up, but with time the best we could wish was that they were alive, wherever they were. A few weeks later, for reasons unknown, the Chinese released three of the party, Lt McDonald and Cpls Buckland and Buck, but Ptes Light and Hollis were fated to spend two years under horribly inhumane conditions in a North Korean prison camp.

We were to discover later that while the group was attempting to return to the company position at Ichon they became aware of Chinese soldiers on the road in front of them. They backed off and hid in a hut, but unfortunately this move was observed by a civilian who

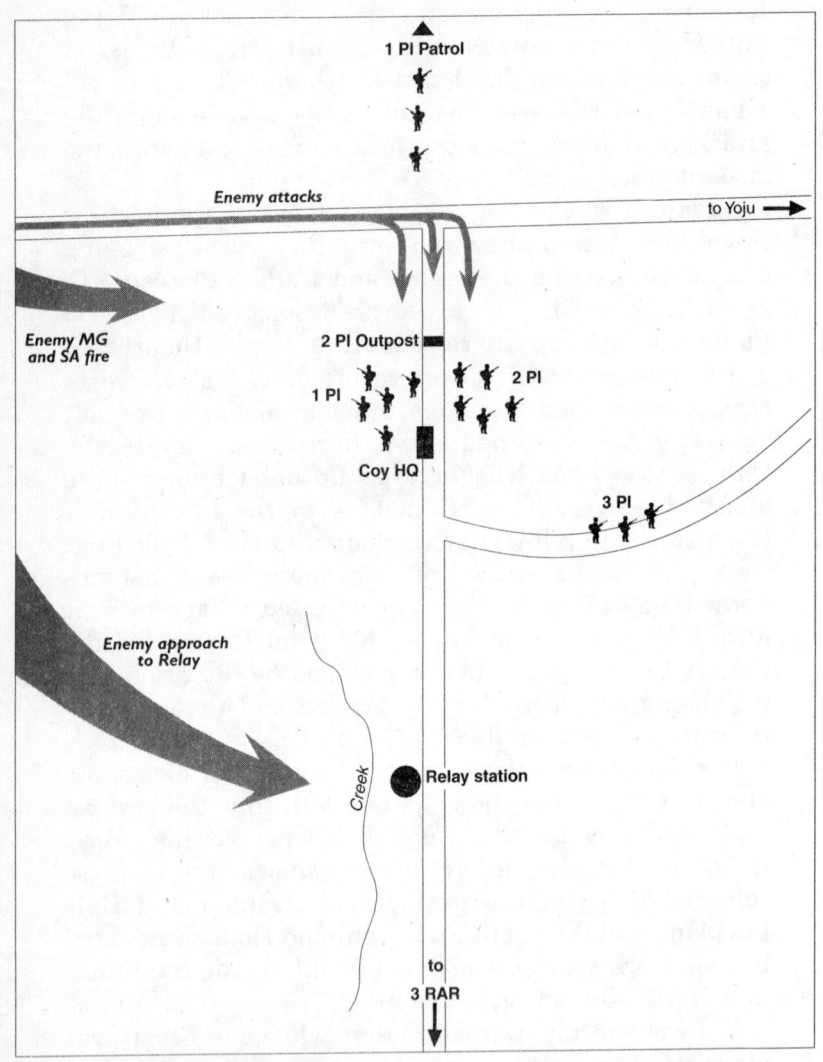

Map 9: Enemy attacks at Ichon

informed the Chinese. The hut was surrounded and the whole patrol taken prisoner.

I was surprised that they had even contemplated returning to the company position with all the noise of battle and the spraying of tracer warning of the enemy on our doorstep. Circumstances should have dictated avoiding that area, even if I had not ordered it.

To site a patrol in "no man's land" nineteen kilometres from friendly troops, and in close proximity to enemy defences, will always be a risky business.To repeat this seven nights in succession is provoking any red-blooded enemy commander worth his salt to take a shot at destroying it. I have absolutely no doubt that the trap was being set for us that night and it might have worked had we not observed the force going around us, silhouetted against a background of snow.We beat the trap by no more than five minutes. Further delay of the initial withdrawal would have resulted in the relay station group being wiped out and the main body ambushed. The inevitable result would have been men killed and wounded a long way from home, for no useful purpose.There was nothing we could have done to avert the fate of McDonald's patrol.

Many years ago I caught up with one of the men taken prisoner on this patrol, Tom Hollis, and learnt the details of their capture. Jack Gallaway recorded the following account:

> We went down to where the village started and went into a hut to check out the maps and where we were going. This hut was full of young men in Korean clothing. There would have been at least fifteen of them. I thought after, they were most likely Chinese in Korean clothing.[4]
>
> We went to our right around the valley until we got to the mountains on the other side. This would have taken us around four hours. The snow was up to your crutch where the wind drifts were and it was very hard to get through. We realised we would have to move rather swiftly, otherwise we wouldn't get back before daylight.
>
> We moved right around and got to the foot of the valley

on the other side. We stopped for a smoke, then climbed the
mountain. It was quite a large mountain, much larger than
the one the company was on.

We finally came to the top, and as we came to the top of
it the wind nearly blew us off. I looked back and said, "The
boys are having a bit of fun." You could see the machine-gun
fire ... the tracers from Vickers guns and that ... crossed
lines of fire. I was sure there was contact. You don't fire
Vickers guns for fun ... those blokes weren't trigger happy.

With that we moved over the mountain. The other side of
the mountain the snow was up to your waist and it was so
steep that you slipped all the way down ... grabbing saplings.

We got to the bottom and believed that the road ran
straight ahead. We had instructions to cross over the road,
climb the mountain again and back around the other side
of the valley to the company lines.

We couldn't find the road ... it took a left hand turn ... it
didn't go straight ahead, the map was wrong.

We got to this little creek that was covered in ice and
Angus looked across the paddy field and saw these two
houses. He said, "Tom, lead out for those two houses."

So I led out and got there ... this was the first time I was
forward scout. The houses were full of Chinese, you could
hear them snoring, and the sig wire ran up the hill.

There was a bit of an embankment there and we finally
got up the embankment by pushing one man up and pulling
him with a rifle ... Angus had a rifle. We made it to the top
of the mountain, following the sig line all the way and there
was a big dug-out, Japanese style ... they were snoring in
that too.

We did not disturb them and came down off the mountain
and followed the valley around to the village of Ichon and
by this time a couple of the boys were pretty badly distressed.
So when we got back to the little town, I was in the middle
... I was trying to keep the blokes at the rear, Buckland and
Light, up within contact of Buck and McDonald. Angus was
going at a pretty fair bat and I was trying to keep up. I
said: "We'll have to take the high ground back into the
company, Angus. These blokes will never get up the
mountain."

It was a pretty steep mountain up to that position and I
suggested that we go to the left and follow the low ground

and swing in behind the company. From O'Dowd's account I'm pleased we didn't. Angus disagreed and said we would have to follow the high ground. I said, "What about we bowl straight up the centre of the village?" He said, "Lead off."

So I did. Halfway through, I put my hand up because I could see someone in front of me and at that time someone turned off to their right and there were about sixty of them and we realised we were following a Chinese patrol.

We ran back the way we had come. There was a little round dug-out and we dropped in to that and that was where we decided what we were going to do.

We decided to work our way back into the village on the top side where the high ground was. The same way the Chinese had gone. I thought that this was a bit ridiculous but I wasn't in charge.

We got halfway through the village and decided to pull up and have a blow and we moved into a hut. We reckoned we'd wait until first light and see what was happening. There was no fire from the company position and by this time I estimated it would have been three o'clock, but it has been estimated that it was four or half past by that time because it was quite light. With the snow that was always the case.

This hut had two rooms. I checked the first room and collared a Korean there, but no one checked the second room. By the time we got in there and closed the door I heard a door close, but by the time I looked out there was nothing there. So this guy apparently went and got the Chinese. A couple of the men had taken their boots off to warm their feet on the floor.

Buck was sitting at the front of the house watching the door and I was at the back door. Angus asked me to look for a way out. I looked out not realising with the snow on the rise that there was something like an eight-foot wall at the back. I said "No problem" and went out and ran straight into the wall and bounced off. Angus got on top of the wall and from there he could see how many Chinese were around us.

The Chinese came through the door and when we looked around they had set up a machine-gun and all outside the hut. I estimated there were sixty of them and they were right round us. They disarmed us and made us carry all the empty weapons.

I don't know what the instructions were to the company, but I think they were long gone by the time we got back.

THIRTEEN
PATROL TO CHIPYONG-NI

On 22 January Gen Ridgway ordered a general advance in I, IX and X Corps which was well under way by the 25th. The Commonwealth Brigade was in corps reserve, and on the 31st moved into the town of Changhowon-ni. Here the battalions were deployed in a deserted village. I was again accommodated in a deserted Korean hut, and as we were well out of the action, a fairly relaxed atmosphere developed.

I had endeavoured to maintain the company at a fighting strength, sufficient to take casualties without the danger of becoming too weak to continue. By this time numbers had been so reduced as to cause me concern. Previous operations and general attrition had taken their toll, and reinforcements were not forthcoming. For this reason I made the unpopular decision to stop R & R Leave for A Company until we were reinforced.

At this time there was also general dissatisfaction in the ranks about the nature of coverage in the press. The newspapers back in Australia gave little attention to the actions fought or the uncomfortable conditions of daily life. One soldier presented me with a newspaper cutting describing the great time the Diggers were having in Japan on R & R. The journalist's glowing account was supported by photographs of soldiers and Japanese maidens having a jolly old time. In the letter that came with the clipping the soldier's relatives expressed relief that the Korean War was such fun. He was not a happy Digger.

On the same day I had a visit from a war correspondent with whom I was on friendly terms, Ian Reid, a Kiwi by religion who reported for the Melbourne *Herald* and the Sydney *Sun*. Ian opened with, "Great stuff. How about the story, Ben?", and my response was not as friendly as it should have been. He was referring to the unfortunate Ichon patrol and I was still stinging from it. I showed him the newspaper cutting and conveyed the soldiers' sentiments concerning the views it expressed. For good measure I added that, due to lack of reinforcements, I had stopped A Company fron getting R & R leave anyway. I suggested that war correspondents could serve us better if they emphasised the serious activities of the battalion, and the conditions under which the men fought and lived.

Unintentionally I had given him a story. He latched on to the lack of reinforcement bit, researched it and wrote a blistering report which his papers ran. This provoked a descending scale of backside kicking, starting with the Minister for the Army and the Chief of the General Staff and working down through army ranks until it reached our GOC, Gen Robertson. Dear Red Robbie took it badly, and the message was out that he was looking for the pariah's dog to kick. Naturally I kept a very low profile.

Later an obviously elated Ian Reid paid me another visit, this time to offer profuse thanks for the story. He waved a congratulatory telegram from his editor who was in raptures because they had got the pollies hopping. I told him he did not know me, had never met me and in fact had never even heard of me.

But from then reinforcements flowed in a steady stream.

C Company Commander, Arch Denness, was a non-drinker who accumulated his beer ration to share with his friends when things were quiet. In this location we were a long way from the action, so Arch invited Reg and me and a couple of others to come over and assist in disposing of some of the bottles littering his tent. Being fairly cooperative chaps, always willing to help a friend, we agreed, and spent some hours in his company. Returning to our hut I tripped over a body on the floor. Thinking it was some Digger being out of order, I nudged him with the boot and told him to remove himself. The body sprang to attention and in most precise English declared, "Lt F. W. Gardner, sir! Reporting for duty as one of your platoon commanders."

Fred was told to get back to sleep and in the morning a decision would be made about whether he got a platoon. From Freddie's accent it was obvious he had a previous conviction — born in England — and I was not sure that inserting him in to a platoon cold was a good idea. Next morning I had a good look at him and liked what I saw. He had been in the UK Army in World War II serving in Burma as British officer with the Gurkhas. He was wearing a Gurkha kukri which I told him to leave in his haversack until the Diggers got used to him. I gave him 1 Platoon, wondering how his Englishness would go over with the young gentlemen of that platoon, but there was no problem. Nunan's comment was typical, though not very well expressed:

"Skipper, the new officer's a Pom."

"Yes Roy. He was an officer in the British Army."

"He talks with a plum up his bum."

"I think you mean a plum in his mouth."

"No Boss, plum up his bum."

"Go and clean your Owen gun, Roy, it's filthy."

Many Nunan conversations were terminated with the state of his gun. It was a safe bet it required cleaning.

On 6 February the battalion moved to the town of Yoju where most of the company were non-tactically accommodated in Korean huts. Against the possibility of becoming operational, the Orders Group assembled on the Seoul–Yoju road, where defensive positions were allocated and reconnaissance conducted. It was during such a reconnaissance that a US General gave unexpected assistance to two of our men involved in a vehicle accident. Lt John Church was returning to our base when his jeep skidded as he tried to avoid a pothole, and slid off the gravel road, down the embankment and overturned. Church was thrown clear and was unhurt, and he set about assisting his driver, Pte Brien Baker. Church takes up the story:

> As I was doing this, a small reconnaissance helicopter landed beside us on the river bank. The new IX Corps Commander, Maj Gen Bryant Moore, who had seen the accident from on high, hopped out and told me to go and get our RMO to come forward. Don Beard was rather surprised to see me but went back in the helicopter to look after the driver.[1]

This was a nice piece of noblesse oblige by a busy general. Unfortunately, within weeks of this incident Gen Moore was killed when his helicopter crashed.

From where I set up Company Headquarters the view of the wide, frozen Han River was spoiled by the bodies of a few dead enemy soldiers lying frozen on it. A platoon was detailed to smash the ice, push them under and give them an icy entombment.

The adjutant of the Argylls was Capt John Slim, son of Field Marshal Sir William Slim. John and Fred Gardner were old friends from their days together in a Gurkha regiment during the Burma War. Slim often dropped in to chat. In this location we took advantage of the opportunity to let Cpl Robinson and his cooks, Muncy and Taylor, excel themselves with some culinary delights, and invited Slim along for the occasion.

Meanwhile, the US 23rd RCT, with the French Battalion and considerable artillery support, occupied a perimeter about twenty-four kilometres north of Yoju, at Chipyong-ni. The French Battalion was commanded by Lt Col Monclar who had busted himself from Lt Gen to Lt Col for the privilege of taking this battalion to Korea. The 23rd RCT perimeter was attracting active attention from the Chinese, who were executing a workmanlike job on an encircling movement. The Corps Commander had approved plans to extract the RCT but Gen Ridgeway directed otherwise. Sticking with the aggressive policy he had enunciated on assuming command, he directed there would be no withdrawal; they would stand and fight.

One of 3 RAR's routine daily tasks was to dispatch a company-strength fighting patrol through to 23 RCT, to confirm that the road was still open. On the morning of the 13th it was A Company's turn to provide this clearing patrol and, as it transpired, the last.

Apart from an artillery FOO I do not remember other attachments, but no doubt Support Company was represented by Mortars or MMGs, or both. The company was mounted in GMCs and set off along the Chipyong-ni road early on a warm, sunny morning. Our first stop was to check in at a Divisional Forward Tactical Headquarters a few kilometres along and to the left of the road. The operations staff there were very subdued, gloomily conveying an impression of gaining little joy from the way events were shaping. They could tell me nothing about the situation on the road ahead, so the patrol continued.

The only enemy contact came about a kilometres further along the road and out to the left, where we sighted an enemy group of about ten men. The Diggers opened fire and after some confusion the enemy disappeared into the bush. There was talk of taking off after them but I stopped this. Our task was to check out the road and this would not be done if we got caught up in sideshows along the way. There were one or two other minor sightings well out to the left, but nothing in the vicinity of the road which might offer a threat to communications.

Arriving inside the perimeter I reported to the RCT Operations Officer regarding the incidents along the road. He briefed me on his marked-up operations map,

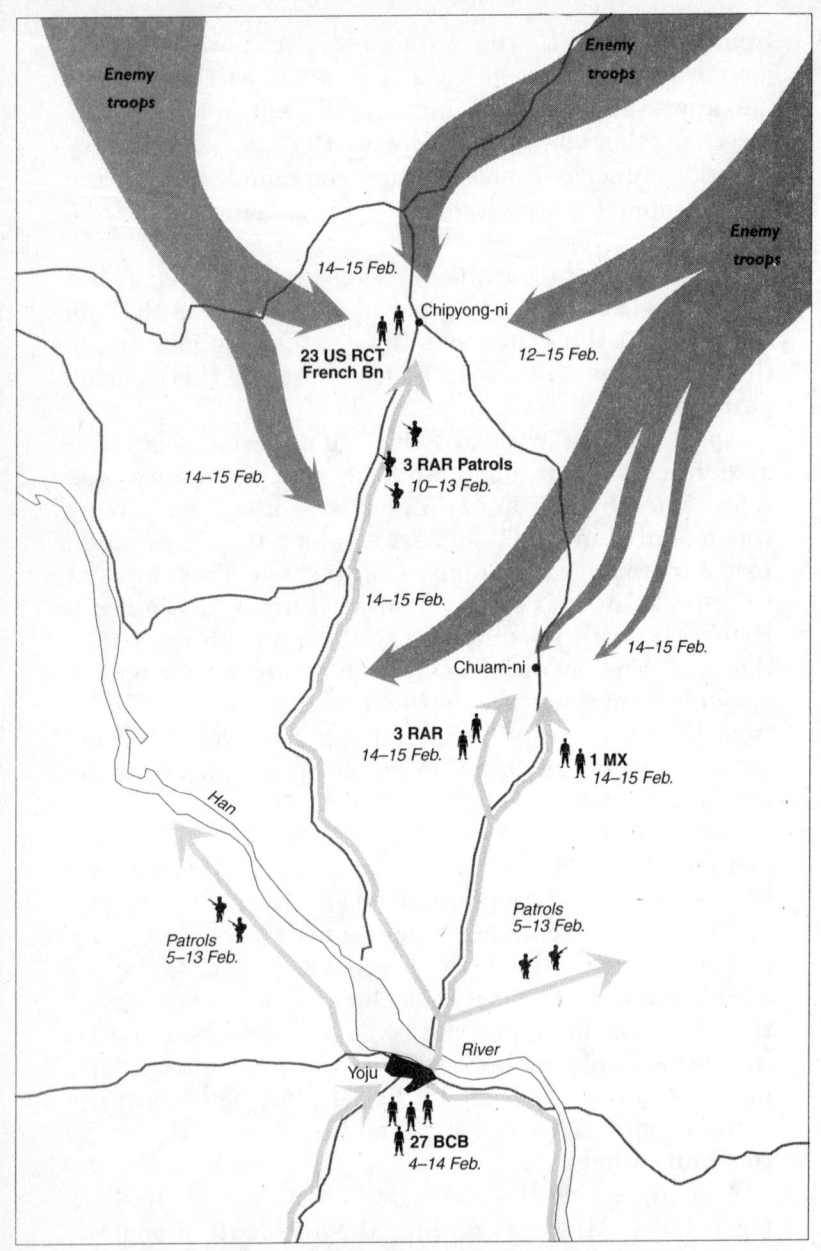

Map 10: 3 RAR movements, 4–15 February 1951. Attack on "Doctor"

A Company headquarters, late March 1951. Front row, 3rd from left is the CSM, Tom Muggleton, and 5th from left is the unmistakable Capt Reg Saunders. (Author's collection)

1 Platoon, late March 1951. (Author's collection)

2 Platoon, late March 1951. In the middle in the front row is Sgt George Harris, at that time platoon commander. (Author's collection)

3 Platoon, late March 1951. In the back row, 2nd from left is Lt Harold Mulry. (Author's collection)

Some A Company NCOs, late March 1951. Back row: S/Sgt Bill Mann on left, Cpl Jim Everleigh 3rd from left and Snowy Barnes 4th from left. Front row: 2nd, 3rd and 4th from left, Sgt Vic Svenson, CSM Tom Muggleton and Sgt George Harris. (Courtesy Tom Muggleton)

The kind of hard going that had to be overcome in the approach to the attack on Hill 410.

Cpl S. F. (Nobby) Clark,
A Company RAAMC
Medic, sharing a letter.
(Courtesy Nobby Clark)

Cpl S. F. (Nobby) Clark
(with Owen gun) and
Stretcher Bearer Pte A.
K. (Allan) Cardinal.
(Courtesy Nobby Clark)

A Company going in for the attack on Chongju.

A briefing. On left is the IO, Lt Alf Argent, and seated with pointer is Lt Col Ferguson. The company commanders, from the top, are O'Dowd with cigarette, Capt Darcy Laughlin, Maj Arch Denness (bending down), and Maj Wally Brown. (Courtesy Alf Argent)

Ron Perkins (left) with Maj Gen Jim Hughes, November 1998. Sgt Ron Perkins was A Company Mortar MFC at Kapyong. He acted as the author's control radio operator during the withdrawal of the rifle companies. (Author's collection)

Yung Kim Choy. As a boy he attached himself to Doc Beard's RAP as a general duties man. He is a veteran of the Kapyong battle. Now an Australian citizen, he attends all 3 RAR Kapyong parades. (Author's collection)

Left to right: Vic Carr, Sgt Vic Svenson and Cpl Allan (Hoagie) Carmichael, November 1998. (Author's collection)

Mrs Kim Clang Keun with Mrs Olwyn Green, widow of Lt Col Charles Green. Mrs Kim has been placing flowers on the grave of Sgt Vince Healy since the end of the Korean War. (Author's collection)

Tom Hollis, seated, wearing his World War II Commando beret. Behind him is Allan Carmichael. (Author's collection)

Sgts Lennie Lenoy and Jim Stark share something to keep out the cold. Lennie was killed at Kapyong, manning his MMG. (AWM accession no. PO1813.866. Robinson photograph)

Capt Reg Saunders, centre, with RSM Bill Harrison and Pte (Alby) Alberts of Battalion HQ. (AWM accession no. PO1813.467)

South Korean porters carry supplies to A Company on Hill Sardine. (AWM accession no. PO1813.523)

Moving to the start line for the attack on Sardine, A Company stand aside to permit the evacuation of Middlesex wounded. (AWM accession no. PO1813.450)

WOII Tom Muggleton, CSM of A Company. (Courtesy Jack Gallaway)

Centre: Capt Norman Gravener who commanded D Company at Kapyong. On the left, holding a pole, is Mr Robinson, the Salvation Army representative. On the right is Fr Joe Phillips. (Courtesy Jack Gallaway)

Lt John Church, commander of 2 Platoon and wounded at Chisan. (AWM accession no. PO1813.511. Robertson photograph)

Sergeant A. R. Robinson, A Company cook, having problems with the US Army Thanksgiving rations. He had a number of turkeys to cook. (AWM accession no. 147001)

Fr Joe Phillips celebrating Mass in the field on an altar improvised from a stretcher and an army blanket. (AWM accession no. PO1813.457. Robertson photograph)

Padre Laing conducting a Church of England service in a paddy field. Again, the altar was constructed from an army blanket draped over a stretcher. (AWM accession no. PO1813.458. Robertson photograph)

Lt Col Green introducing Brig Coad to officers. The officer on the right of the photograph is Lt L. G. (Algy) Clark, who took command of A Company at the Battle of Pakchon. (AWM accession no. 146906. Holzheimer photograph)

The innocent victims of war, the refugees — women, old men and children. Where they would get their next meal or spend the night did not bear thinking about. (AWM accession no. PO1813.422. Robertson photograph)

Pte E. J. (Bomber) Brown, wounded in the attack on Hill Sardine but still dangerous. (AWM accession no. 147334. Holzheimer photograph)

The Argyll and Sutherland Highlanders lead out for their long march from Kunuri with bagpiper setting the pace. (AWM accession no. PO1813.479. Robertson photograph)

From left: Cpl Jim Everleigh who served A Company so aggressively and well, Pte Ted Pearson, and O'Dowd's orderly, Pte Roy Nunan. (AWM accession no. PO2208.009. Shelton photograph)

Soldiers trying to smash their way into frozen ground to carve out a weapons pit to fight from. (AWM accession no. PO1813.565. Robertson photograph)

The A Company radio operator on the command net, Pte Brian (Lofty) Heweston. No matter what the radio or the conditions, Lofty got "through". Note the American tankie asleep on the Sherman. (AWM accession no. PO1813.452. Robertson photograph)

2nd Lt Don Scott, Royal New Zealand Artillery. At the Battle of Kapyong "Scottie" was the Forward Observation Officer who put down fire on the Battalion's left flank. In all likelihood, his action prevented the enemy from establishing a blocking position and preventing the withdrawal of the rifle companies.

which displayed the known enemy positions in thick red pencil, along with red arrows for enemy attacks and probing actions. I took particular note that the red arrows were getting perilously close to the sides of the road of our withdrawal route.

Also displayed on his map was an isolated US Army detachment out to the east on the Chuam-ni to Chipyong-ni road. For this unfortunate little group the red pencil told of an even more alarming situation. I was informed that this was an outpost position held by the 2 Division Reconnaissance Company and L Company (of 9 Regiment), and the operations staff were working on a plan to extract them. I refrained from offering some tempting odds about their chance of success.

With the red pencil's message of closing jaws in mind, we mounted and took to the road, all eyes searching the edges for signs of trouble, but the return journey was uneventful.

FOURTEEN

ATTACK ON HILL 195, "DOCTOR"

There were no surprises in the reports next morning, 14 February. The Chinese had completely invested 23 Regimental Combat Team and the French Battalion, and had them heavily under attack.

The really bad news was the fate of L Company and the Div Recon. The Chuam-ni road ran north–south through a valley dominated by a low ridge on either side, an obvious and tempting ambush situation. It was on these ridges that the Chinese set up business with machine-guns and mortars. The unfortunate Div Recon and L Company attempted to run the valley in a vehicle convoy, and the inevitable result was a massacre.

Corps Headquarters reaction to the Chipyong-ni situation was to attempt a break-through to the 23 RCT by attacks from two directions, one along the Chipyong-ni road which had previously been 3 RAR's daily patrol route. The break-through was to be executed by US tanks and infantry, following a massive artillery and air preparation. The Chuam-ni valley drive was to be made by 27 British Commonwealth Brigade attacking up the road on which the Div Recon and L Company had just been butchered.

27th Brigade moved immediately to the mouth of the valley and commenced movement along the high ground on either side, the Middlesex Regiment leading. About a kilometre in, the Middlesex were fired upon by an enemy force dug in on the high ground on the right of the road. The Regiment mounted a successful attack and later, during the night, beat off the inevitable counter-attack, inflicting very heavy casualties on the enemy in the process.

From there 3 RAR took the lead, with a company clearing the high ground on each side of the road, C Company on the right and B Company on the left. B Company was successful, but the enemy on the right of the road held firm, and C Company could make no headway. The next day, the 15th, the CO ordered an assault on Hill 195, code-named "Doctor". The initial plan was for a two-company attack. B Company was to secure A Company's right flank by clearing the high ground on the right (east) of the road. On the left of the road A Company was to attack Hill 195.

Hill 195 was a nasty looking feature, broad, bald, and devoid of any form of cover. It rose gently from a gully to its crest, providing an excellent, unimpeded field of fire for the enemy throughout its entire length. There was no room for flanking, no option but to approach straight uphill into the enemy's fire, in Digger parlance "up the guts". We preferred the suspicious-husband tactic — knock on the front door and run around the back. It was apparent that success for this attack would depend on devastating mortar and artillery preparation. An accurate aircraft strafing and bombing run would have been a great help.

I worked with the NZ Artillery Forward Observation Officer and the US 4.2 inch Mortar Fire Controller during ranging for support, but a gremlin crept into the process. Ranging rounds from the 25-pounders would register on the crest of 195, but any attempt to establish a bracket produced a muffled sound, as if most of the shot was landing kilometres beyond the objective. A test of "gun fire" produced only a few rounds on the objective, the remainder disappearing into the distance. Experiment as we might a satisfactory barrage could not be achieved. The 4.2 inch mortar registration gave the same result. It was clear there would be no devastating artillery preparation for this attack. Eventually, about mid-afternoon, the CO gave up and ordered the attack to go ahead anyway.

In addition to the enemy on the ridge on the right side the road I foresaw another problem. On the left of 195, a long ridge about the same height extended north–south, parallel to our objective. This ridge had not been cleared and I suggested to the CO that if there were enemy on it they would have us in range and in enfilade. He assured me it was clean, and as I was in no position to question the source of this piece of intelligence, I had to accept it as such.

Having the furthest to go, B Company started off first, dispatching a platoon to secure their forming-up place and start line for the advance on the right of the road. This platoon immediately came under fire from machine-guns and mortars from that direction. The remainder of B Company was then committed but could make no progress. It was now clear that the enemy on the right of the road was there in strength and Col Ferguson abandoned this part of the program and pulled B Company out.

A Company now had to go it alone with an exposed right flank, the Chinese across the road having nothing to distract their attention from our attack. Ineffective artillery support and an insecure right flank gave this operation little chance of success from the outset.

It was about 1630 when we arrived at the creek bed which was our start line. I arranged the company in the gully without difficulty and waited while our artillery and mortars banged away in accordance with the program. However, we had little confidence in the effect this would have, knowing that the moment we became exposed the enemy would make life very uncomfortable indeed, from both the front and right flanks. This would persist throughout progress up the hill to the point where a final charge could be made. I began to appreciate how the Light Brigade must have felt when ordered to do their equestrian party piece.

To disperse the enemy fire I adopted a broad, open formation on a two-platoon front; on the left was Freddie Gardner's 1 Platoon, on the right John Church's 2 Platoon, with Harold Mulry's 3 Platoon following in reserve. As anticipated, casualties were taken early, and the enemy continued to exact a toll as the Diggers progressed towards the crest of the feature. About halfway to the objective the company began to take rifle and machine-gun fire in enfilade from the parallel ridge on our left (so much for it being clean) as well as from across the road on our right. The air was thick with the snap and whine of bullets and the crump of enemy mortars' bombs. Fortunately a lot of the flanking fire was high, but enough was on target to take casualties.

John Church attempted a right flanking movement with 2 Platoon[1] with a group under command of the acting platoon sergeant, Cpl Jack Sheppard, MM,[2] but they ran into intense fire, which killed Sheppard and pinned the section down. The company continued to engage the enemy with machine-gun, rifle and 2 inch mortar fire while I brought the US 4.2 Mortar FOO forward to recheck his registration and lay down a barrage. This bombardment appeared to be a little more effective, so platoon commanders were ordered to give it another push. They and their remarkable men carried us to about the three-quarters mark. Tom Muggleton and I could clearly see the enemy by this time, but that was it. There was too much small-arms fire coming from all sides and further progress was absolutely impossible without taking unacceptable casualties. It was now late afternoon and the battlefield was littered with the dead and wounded. Enemy fire was so effective that we could move neither forward nor back. I reported this situation

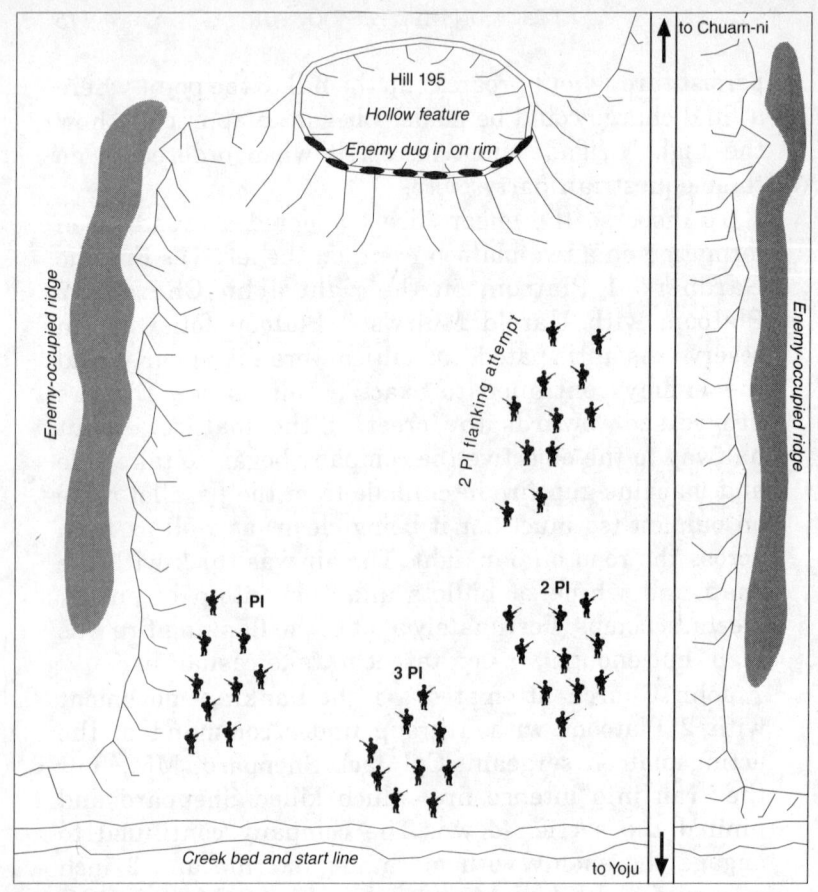

Map 11: "Doctor" battlefield

to the CO and he called off the attack, giving me approval to withdraw.[3]

With the enemy in command of the battlefield, withdrawal of the company as a whole had to wait until dusk. However, the wounded were somehow passed to the rear by their mates and Nobby Clark's dedicated stretcher-bearers. This battle cost A Company three men killed and fifteen wounded.

While we were fighting to take "Doctor", relief of the Chipyong-ni perimeter was effected.

During the night of the 14th the Chinese Communist Force drove into the Chipyong-ni defences, making serious inroads, in one place as far as the gun lines. To recover the situation a force of twenty-three tanks was employed with 160 infantry mounted on them. The force drove through the Chinese lines to the beleaguered US Regiment and French Battalion. Of the 160 infantry mounted on the tanks only twenty-three remained with the tanks when they arrived in the perimeter, and thirteen of these were wounded. My mind went back to the operation in January, when A Company was scheduled for a similar tank-mounted debacle.

No major action was seen by 3 RAR on 16 February. A soldier of D Company was killed by machine-gun fire. On reconnaissance, the C Company commander, Capt John Callander, and the Anti-Tank platoon sergeant, Sgt Dowsett, were wounded by a round from a mountain gun.

On the 17th air reports indicated that the enemy was retreating on all fronts, so Col Ferguson told me to repeat the attack on 195. We went through the same procedure as on the 15th, but without support, and reached the objective unopposed. The reason for the artillery and mortar ranging problems became apparent. The map did not show it but the crest of 195 was hollowed out; it looked like a small volcano crater with a narrow, two-metre rim around it. It was on this narrow rim that the enemy had dug their weapon pits, commanding our approach all the way up the slope. Only a lucky shot from the supporting arms could hit a weapon pit; the rounds falling below the rim were ineffective, and those going over disappeared harmlessly into the hollow, with the muffled thump giving the impression of landing miles away.

There were eleven enemy dead on the crest, seven of whom had been shot in the head by our small-arms fire. In defence, the head is the only target offered by the enemy so this result spoke well for the Digger's shooting.

From the objective we had a good view of the road leading up the Chuam-ni valley. As far as could be seen it was littered with the vehicles and bodies of the Div Recon and L Company. Reg Saunders, Tom Muggleton and I climbed down to the road for a closer look. Bodies of US soldiers lay on either side of the road or projected from the vehicles and trailers. All were denuded of socks and boots. The Chinese Army footwear was not up to the continuous marching demands of their commanders and the savage Korean winter. For these tough Chinese soldiers, obtaining a pair of the first-class American boots and socks must have been like winning the lottery.

On the side of the road I found the end of a length of signal cable running parallel to it. I followed the cable until it terminated in the middle of the road where an anti tank mine was dug in. It is probable that sighting the mine halted the convoy, giving the enemy a sitting shot the length of it. Making sure the area was clear I had the pleasure of pulling the cable, causing a nice big bang and opening the road.

Following the mid-February battles the Chinese went into another of their unpredictable withdrawal modes. They withdrew leaving delaying forces on carefully selected features, tactical locations where they could impose maximum casualties and delay the following United Nations forces. In our sector it involved chasing them up the Chuam-ni valley and into the mountain it led to. Normally the allies had been road-bound due to supply problems, but Ridgway now issued the order to go after the Chinese in the hills.

In mid-February the 2nd Battalion of the Princess Patricia's Canadian Light Infantry (PPCLI) joined us, making a four-infantry-battalion brigade. The Canadians (known as the Princess Pats) looked distinctive and warm with their Eskimo-style fur lined hood on their parkas.

They were a welcome addition. Like the New Zealanders, the Indians and ourselves they had a British tradition and system of operating. We understood and trusted each other.

FIFTEEN

ATTACK ON HILL 410, "WOODBINE"

On 3 March 1951 the 27th British Commonwealth Brigade again came under the command of 1st US Cavalry Division, for Operation Woodbine, a broad-front attack to push the United Nations line further north. In our sector 3 RAR was ordered to capture ground in the vicinity of Hill 410, in conjunction with the Princess Pats on the left and an ROK battalion on the right. D Day was set for 6 March. Operation Woodbine required formations to leave the road and go after the Chinese on their own ground, in the hills. This called for a change in administration. Store dumps were to be established at a road head from which the resupply of the brigade would be by Korean porter trains, similar to the system we used in World War Two, in New Guinea.

Hill 410 was part of a long ridge running east–west and parallel with the one B Company had just taken, hill 587. The two features were separated by a deep, wide valley through which ran the Asi-ri–Pun Suon road. From the objective on 410 two spurs dropped sharply to the road in the valley. My instructions were to attack up the east (right) spur to gain a footing at its crest. D Company (Capt Bill Keys) would then pass through us to turn west and attack along the ridge to consolidate on 410, the peak of the west spur.[1]

Although early March, the ground was still covered

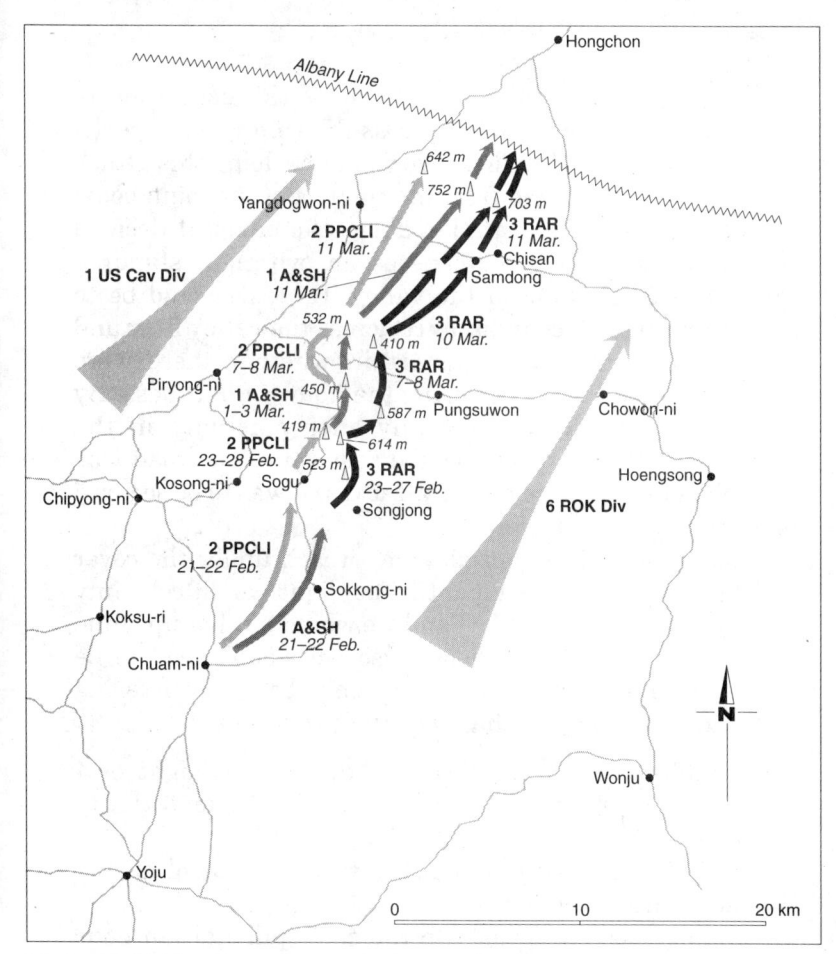

Map 12: 3 RAR movements, 12 February–11 March 1951

with a generous blanket of snow on the hill peak and sides. The days were fine, but the nights were bitterly cold.

When the CO gave me the task he could provide absolutely no enemy information beyond that of a US Air Force report of general strafing of dug-in positions along the ridge line. Clearly the operation involved A company descending the sharp forward slope of 587 in full view of the enemy, crossing the wide valley floor, and climbing the steep approach of the east spur to launch the attack. Looking across the valley to the peaks on the other side, I realised we would be doing this attack on our own, separated from the comfort of the main body.

To gain some information about the enemy I decided to locate one of my platoons as an overnight standing patrol in the bottom of the valley. Its task would be to carry out night reconnaissance across the valley floor and up to the east spur to ascertain whether there were listening posts forward during the hours of darkness. By day they were to observe any enemy activity in the vicinity of the road and on the east spur. The road was the obvious start line for the attack, and was to be secured by the standing patrol.

I considered it essential we approach under the cover of darkness. Any movement in daylight would certainly be observed by the enemy, and we would be shot up while exposed on the valley floor. Also we would need to be well up the spur before the enemy began wandering abroad. I decided on the following programme:

- Establish the standing patrol during the night of 4 March, to obtain some information of enemy activity in the area.
- Move the company to join the standing patrol during the night of the 5th.
- Launch a silent attack up the east spur half an hour before first light on the 6th.

From the map the east ridge appeared to be narrow, dictating a one-platoon front. I nominated Lt Fred Gardner's 1 Platoon to lead the attack, with Lt Harold Mulry's 3 Platoon backing up. Lt John Church's 2 Platoon would be the reserve, so logically they were allocated the nasty standing patrol task.

On schedule, 2 Platoon slipped over the side of 587 after last light on the 4th and established a base in the timbered edge of the south side of the road. John Church tasked Cpl Lisk's 5 Section for the reconnaissance patrol with the Platoon Sergeant, George Harris, in command. The patrol climbed the east spur and reached a point halfway up without contact, which was encouraging. They then crossed to the west spur and again found no evidence of the enemy. Returning via the valley floor the patrol froze when a magnesium flare was suddenly lit, illuminating the Chinese soldier on the road who was holding it and peering around. One Digger was tempted to take a shot but was restrained. It was essential to preserve secrecy about our presence in the valley. Lisk's patrol continued on, freezing each time a flare was lit. On return the patrol reported its findings and 2 Platoon remained on "stand to" until dawn.[2]

Why the flares? It was obvious the enemy had no idea of our presence in the area, or they would not have exposed themselves in this manner. My guess is that they were either a signal to a commander elsewhere or they indicated a rendezvous point for enemy troops out on missions that night.

During daylight 2 Platoon was well concealed by the timber line. Church was able to observe considerable enemy movement up and down the valley road, and on the two spurs opposite, but no attempt was made to approach the southern side of the road.

The US Engineer project to construct a road to the brigade supply base got behind schedule, causing the attack to be postponed for twenty-four hours. This was bad news for 2 Platoon, stuck in close proximity to the enemy and a long way from support. After last light I dispatched Reg Saunders and his batman to join them. There were two reasons for sending Reg. The information I needed to convey to Church was such that it should not be put over the air in "clear". One had to assume that the enemy could read our radio transmissions, whether that was the case or not. Secondly, the platoon was in a nerve-racking position and some moral support by a visit from the headquarters could do no harm. Reg was to explain the changed situation and plan and instruct Church to stay put until I brought the company down after last light on the 6th, preparatory to a pre-dawn attack on the 7th.[3]

After last light on 6 March the company embarked on its approach down the steep track to the road. 2 Platoon's descent two nights previously had churned the snow to slush which, by now, had frozen to an icy surface. The slippery surface and steep gradient rendered it impossible to maintain footing, causing men to slide downhill in a confused melee. To stand was to be knocked down by the soldier behind loosing his footing. There was constant danger as men lost control of heavy items. Light and Medium Machine Guns, their tripods, boxes of ammunition and so on hurtled past us alarmingly, with brief warning from those above. Eventually we all resorted to sliding along on our backsides. Since that night the Diggers have identified this operation as the "Slippery Slide".

In due course the company sorted itself out at the bottom of the hill and moved on to join 2 Platoon. Church and his platoon had been through an uncomfortable experience, to say the least, stuck way out on their own, constantly in a state of "stand to". The enemy would certainly have made trouble had their presence been discovered. The original intention had been to leave them in position for one night with the company joining them the next. As it turned out, we could not join them until the third night. This situation required the steadiness and leadership that John Church and his NCOs provided.

I was advised that the enemy did not appear to be dug in below the 410 ridge but did have an unobstructed view down the steep east spur and into the wide valley floor. This made it certain we would be shot up and mortared if we emerged from the timber line in daylight, taking casualties all the way across the valley floor to the cover of the timber line on the opposite side. Their observation of our approach route and reports of enemy movement on the valley floor in daylight hours confirmed my view that our approach had to be made in darkness, before their patrols ventured forth. It was my intention to make a silent approach up the east ridge, with the hope of jumping the enemy before dawn.

Well before daylight we got under way and successfully crossed the road with 1 Platoon leading, deployed as wide as the narrow ridge would permit, my headquarters close behind. It was breaking first light when the platoon put in its first attack. This was met by mortar, machine-gun and rifle fire emanating from two points, one directly ahead and the other from the adjoining west spur (410) crest. Any exposure greater than fifty centimetres above ground level invited a hail of small-arms fire from these points, and casualties soon mounted.

At this time I noticed that Lofty Heweston, my command net 128 set operator, was not with me. Ossie Osbaldiston, my company net operator, informed me that Lofty had hurt his back in a fall the previous night, and was having difficulties climbing the hill. My instruction was simple: "Go back and help him." Ossie took a long, hard look at me. It was obvious he did not like the order. He was a big man who found it difficult to make himself inconspicuous in circumstances where the least movement drew fire. However, this good soldier slithered out backwards and brought Lofty up for me.

The situation was bogging down and I looked for some way of flanking. The ridge broadened out in the upper reaches and there seemed to be less enemy fire emanating from the right. This appeared to offer possibilities so I instructed Harold Mulry to work the right flank with a hook. He brought 3 Platoon forward and moved to that flank, but immediately drew heavy fire, and with it casualties, including their Platoon Sergeant Charlie Scholl, who was wounded. Sgt Vince Healy and Pte Learmonth (Medium Machine Gun Platoon attached to A Company) ignored the extreme danger of the situation and went forward to rescue their old friend. In the process

Vince was killed and Learmonth wounded. "Greater love hath no man ..."

I aborted the hook.

We were too close to try 25-pounder fire so I brought the US 4.2 Mortar Fire Controller up and told him to get fire on the enemy without including us in the bracket. He did manage to hit the top of the feature but some ranging bombs came uncomfortably close. I took the risk and sent a barrage of bombs across the crest, then increased range, telling Gardner and Mulry to give it another push. They got to their feet and tried again but the enemy fire was still far too accurate and the gradient too steep. We were stuck.

I felt very lonely at this time looking across the valley and up the feature opposite where Battalion HQ and the other rifle companies were still located. I told the CO that we could go no further without incurring an unacceptable level of casualties. He instructed me to hold in our present location while Capt Bill Keys worked the adjoining west spur with D Company.

Bill Keys registered artillery on to his spur so that its range could be increased as his company advanced, providing continuous support ahead of him. They descended from 587, presumably down the slide. Their progress was observed by the enemy and, predictably, when they reached the valley floor the Chinese opened fire with mortars and machine-guns. With the NZ guns engaging the enemy positions, 11 Platoon led the way across, and got a lodgement on the spur without casualties. The other two platoons and company headquarters were not so fortunate, taking several casualties in the crossing process.

During D Company's approach we maintained fire on the enemy in front of us, to hold their attention in our direction.

D Company continued up their spur, staying close under the lifting barrage until the point was reached where employment of artillery was no longer possible.

By this time 11 Platoon was in a position to strike. On that spur the ridge widened out towards the top permitting supporting fire from 10 and 12 Platoons, while 11 Platoon launched a successful attack.

Over in A Company we felt the pressure easing in front of us as D Company closed in and I ordered another push. 1 and 3 Platoons responded with another charge, capturing the crest.[4] Harold Mulry had reported that a machine-gun had been harassing them for some time. Cpl Carmichael's section got a line on the gun's position when enemy grenades were tossed from it during their charge. Carmichael responded with a 36 grenade and his Bren gunner, Pte Bert Bewley, got on top of the weapon pit and fired into it. For his troubles Carmichael was wounded in the face.

The loss of Charlie Scholl was covered by Cpl H. L. P. Smith taking over as Platoon Sergeant.

For both companies this was a bad day out by any measure — twelve men killed and thirty-one wounded. Unfortunately one does not get a second shot at planning an attack, which no doubt is why we are supposed to get it right the first time. However, with the perception of hindsight what can we learn from this operation?

Relying on darkness to conceal our intentions until the last minute in order to get the soldiers close enough to jump the enemy was not a good decision on my part. We crossed the valley floor and made three-quarters of the spur without casualties — I got that much right. But without a solid thrashing from artillery to soften the enemy, the final push right under the enemy guns was not possible. I made a firm resolution that in preparation of any future attack I would blast the top off the objective with every ounce of high explosive available to me, and throw in smoke, if applicable.

Fire and movement is applicable at every level. By approaching alone, all enemy resources, from both crests, were brought to bear on A Company. A plan for a two company attack coordinated by battalion headquarters would have been more effective. Accurate artillery preparation with A and D companies attacking simultaneously up the parallel ridges would have produced better results. The enemy fire power could have been split while we supported each other forward. I believe by this method there would have been fewer casualties.

Sgt Vince Healy had made the supreme sacrifice when attempting to rescue his wounded friend, Sgt Charlie Scholl. At the conclusion of the war Vince's mother made a trip to Korea, to visit his grave. As she placed flowers and a set of rosary beads on the grave, a Korean woman, Kim Clang Keun, witnessed the sad incident and was touched by the mother's grief. Since that day Mrs Kim has visited Vince's grave at regular intervals to lay flowers on it. Through Mrs Olwyn Green, the widow of Lt Col Charles Green, and the Royal Australian Regiment Foundation, Mrs Kim was brought to Australia for a visit, and I had the good fortune to meet her at the Kapyong Day Ceremonial Parade in April 1999.

SIXTEEN

THE GOD BOTHERERS

During the war in the Pacific an American chaplain made the well-publicised statement, "There are no atheists in the foxholes".[1] Looking at some of the magnificent villains in my company I had to conclude that the good chaplain got his sums wrong. There were those who had seen the inside of a church only when (or if) baptised, and had no intention of repeating the experience, baring matrimony. However, morality on the battle field requires the soldier to hold his own life cheaply, in the interest of his comrades. "Greater love hath no man than this ..." On this score they lacked nothing, and could stand proud before their Maker.

Protestants came under the administration of a Church of England chaplain, Padre Laing, a cheerful, friendly soul known generally as "Padre". Catholics were the domain of Father Joe Phillips, who got "Father Joe" from Catholics and Protestants alike. Our Salvation Army Representative, Mr Robertson, provided an ear or shoulder for any denomination. His initials were F. C. but I have no idea what they stood for. He was our well-respected "Mr Robertson", though I have no doubt he also responded to "Robbie".

Church services were arranged on any Sunday when we were not engaged in some territorial dispute with the Chinese Army. A signal originated from Battalion HQ setting out the locations, timings etc. For C of Es, Padre Laing provided a church service in each company area, climbing the hill to the companies in turn. In A Company a suitable space would be selected for his service and platoon commanders briefed to get among the men to encourage attendance.

On the battalion's first Christmas Day, 1950, Padre Laing put a team of carol singers together to visit each rifle company. These familiar, traditional Christmas songs provided an unexpected and welcome touch of home.

Father Joe was not in the general mould of the jovial army priest. He was a tall, pale, slim man, quiet and aesthetic, who nevertheless acquired respect without demanding it. It is unusual to find a Discalced Carmelite priest in the services, but that was Father Phillips' calling. "Discalced" means "no sox", and summer or winter, snow or rain, he wore bare feet inside his boots. Considering the murderous Korean winter this was testimony to his piety ... and toughness.

By the rules existing at that time, Catholic priests were restricted to one Mass per day. The advice from headquarters detailed the location for this Mass and the faithful plodded down to it, trudging back uphill afterwards, an incentive to join Padre Laing's team. Sometimes Fr Joe would conduct Mass in a building, a deserted school or the like, but more often it was in the middle of a paddy field. His batman, Keith Larkin, set up an altar, employing any suitable object which could be disguised to respectability with an army blanket.

Confession preceded Mass for those who had somehow managed to sin. Father Joe sat to one side of the altar on whatever was available, while the penitents knelt in turn before him, to wipe the slate clean. I often think back on those services in the quiet of a paddy field. Apart from the murmur of Latin there was no distraction from reflection on good men no longer with us, what we had survived so far and what we had yet to face. In our modern church, noise is encouraged, and I do not regard it as a sacred experience to sit amidst hundreds of people singing in undisciplined unison and flat.

Mr Robertson also conducted a sincere service at battalion headquarters for his own following. I imagine the OPDs (other Protestant denominations — Methodists, Presbyterian, Baptist etc.) would relate more to him than to Padre Laing or Father Joe.

For tactical reasons rifle companies are always happiest on a high hill. This necessitates the daily resupply of rations, mail, etc. to be lumped up on the backs of carrying parties. Invariably one of the padres or Mr Robertson accompanied each such group, toting their share of the load. While with the company they circulated among the Diggers conversing generally or discussing more intimate matters if a soldier had a personal problem.

I was often intrigued to hear soldiers calling to Padre Laing inquiring after his aunt. I thought concern for his relatives was a nice gesture. One day I discovered the cause of such interest. I was present when someone asked the Padre if he had heard from Auntie recently: Padre waved an envelope in the air.

> "Yes. This came the other day. Aunt is in very good spirits. It seems there has been an American Aircraft Carrier in Sydney Harbour. Auntie says she met up with a bunch of US sailors and gave them a conducted tour of the bright spots of Sydney. In the evening the group retired to the sailors' hotel where they enjoyed some rum and cokes. Poor Auntie doesn't spell very well — she wrote 'rum and coax'."

After that I too took an interest in Auntie's well being, and followed her adventures.

Father Joe had been raised in a racing environment. Through family and other correspondence, he was kept informed of such matters. In his contacts with the soldiers he was able to discuss equestrian and associated matters with those of similar interests. This was to lead to an irritating rumour that he ran a book. I was once confronted directly by a senior officer who claimed that

Father Joe took bets in the confessional. It was hard to be charitable in the face of such stupidity. Father Joe would never consider taking a soldier's money, or anyone else's. In any case, a vow of poverty prohibited him from accumulating worldly goods.

With a little thought the rumour mongers would have realised that it was impossible for even a professional bookie to take bets in Korea. There was no data from which to select winners, lay odds or pay out. There was no radio contact with Australia and the only newspapers came from relatives, arriving far too outdated for such purposes. In any case, soldiers required very little or no money in Korea, as everything was laid on for them. What money they could draw was in Occupation Force BAFVS, a currency useless anywhere but within theatre. And paying out successful bets to dead soldiers or evacuated wounded would have presented a nice problem.

When the rifle companies were committed to battle our padres and Mr Robertson

located themselves at the RAP. There they were at the disposal of Doc Beard and his orderlies, assisting with the care and comfort of the wounded. They were also positioned to administer the appropriate rites for those who died or those in extremes.

3 RAR was fortunate in the provision of its three "God Botherers", the universal tag applied by Australian soldiers to the religious. They worked tirelessly in the interests of the Digger. They were not judgmental and empathy existed between chaplain and soldier. Each in his own way did whatever was possible to add another dimension to the soldiers' war service.

SEVENTEEN

ATTACK ON CHISAN

Reg Saunders and I had the usual OC–2iC arrangement. I did the operations and he the administration. The problem with this state of affairs was that Reg was after my job; he was keen to get command. In accordance with Standard Operating Procedures he was always left out of battle during the advance or attack, but at the conclusion of such operations he would rush eagerly forward and then, with obvious disgust, greet me with: "Are YOU still alive!"

At Chisan I made his day, leaving the field on a stretcher.

Following the Hill 410 affair B and C companies took over up front until 11 March, when A Company was ordered to take Hill 432, near the village of Chisan, in conjunction with an ROK unit attacking on our right flank. (See Map 12, page 121). The attack on Chisan I gave to Church's 2 Platoon. Plodding back from receiving orders for Chisan I was subjected to another of Nunan's observations:

"Boss, I hear tell the Australian soldier has great initiative."

"Yes, Roy."

"They say Australian men are natural-born fighting soldiers."

"Is that so?"

"They say the Australian soldier ain't frightened of nuthin'."

"I see."

"Well, Boss, I'm the bloody exception!"

Reflecting on Roy's confession I concluded that, at some time or other, we all considered ourselves "the bloody exception" and prayed to God it would not show.

Arriving at the start line I found it secured for us by the Argylls, in the shape of my friend Lt Colin Mitchell and a team of his Jocks. He confirmed there were Chinese in the village and that the ROKs had not yet arrived to go in on the left flank with us. Wishing me luck, he left to enjoy a brew of tea his orderly had just advised him of.

John Church's 2 Platoon was allocated the task of taking the village of Chisan. As the attack got under way, an ROK officer appeared, and I endeavoured to interrogate him as to when we might expect his boys to come galloping eagerly into the fray. There was a language difficulty, of course, and I was not getting anywhere with him when a mortar bomb rocketed in, blowing him to pieces, and shooting fragments into my right lung and left calf.

Reg Saunders was on the scene immediately and carried on the operation. But it was not easy, as the Chinese were in a well-dug-in, defensive blocking position. During this attack Lt John Church was also wounded, and Sgt George Harris once again took over 2 Platoon and continued to command it through to mid-April. 2 Platoon drove the enemy off, killing thirty in the process. However, before they could get cover the enemy concentrated fire from four mortars on to them, and the platoon had to withdraw. The A Company casualties were two killed and ten wounded.

The War Diary entry for 11 March gave this account:

A Company commenced moving towards this objective of Hill 435. On reaching the spur at (grid reference) A Company came under small-arms fire from the village of Chisan. 2 Platoon, commanded by Lt J. M. Church, were ordered to capture Chisan. The enemy were well dug in and offered stubborn resistance. 2 Platoon secured their objective though their casualties were relatively heavy. However, the enemy returned accurate mortar fire from an estimated number of four mortars and small-arms fire from high ground on the north. The platoon withdrew to the company position. This situation would not have occurred had the 6 ROK Div attacked on the right flank of the battalion, as they were ordered.

Mick Servos, a member of 6 Section of the attacking 2 Platoon, saw it this way:

On 11 March 1951 2 Platoon of A Company attacked the village of Chisan and the high ground above it, the 432 feature. From the crest of 432 and adjoining crests two spurs ran down to the village, with a gully in between them. It was clear the enemy, from the top of the feature, enjoyed good observation over all the ground we were to operate on. The enemy mortar fire controller was to have a field day.

Our section, 6 Section, got the task of attacking the village at the foothills. The most effective enemy fire came from the right, as we looked up the feature. Less fire came from the centre and left. Our Section Leader, Cpl Jack Bagnell, tried fire and movement by getting our rifle group to manoeuvre right while the Bren machine-gun group held enemy heads down. This did not work and the enemy mortars and small-arms fire from the right caught us in enfilade. Our instructions were that should the tactical situation go wrong we were to withdraw back to the start line. In the present circumstances we were forced to make such a hasty withdrawal.

At this stage the situation was that the top of the feature and the houses were occupied by enemy well dug in. The plan now was that we should launch a Platoon attack, with Bagnall's 6 Sections on the right, Butch McHenry's 4 Section on the left and Ted Lisk's 5 Section providing covering fire down the centre. 6 Section moved out and attacked the right-hand spur but immediately came under intense mortar and small-arms fire. Meanwhile 4 Sections attack came in for the same treatment on the left and could not move forward. To cover the withdrawal 5 Section laid down supporting fire. We acted like Phar Lap and got back to our start line. Mortar fire ensured we conducted this withdrawal at a rapid rate.

The view now taken was that the centre approach in the valley was protected by the two spurs and we would do a platoon attack, up the guts. This time 6 Section was on the right, 4 Section on the left and Platoon HQ centre and 5 Section in reserve Unfortunately Lt John Church, the Platoon Commander, was wounded, but Sgt George Harris kept things going. We were told at the orders group that we had to keep going in spite of heavy mortar fire. 4 Section attacked on the left flank and killed most of their enemy and 6 Section took care of the enemy in the vicinity of the village. On signal, 5 Section joined us. We now continued the attack to the high ground, killing most of the enemy, the remainder running away. In previous operations there had been a tendency to chase the enemy, becoming disorganised. For this operation we were told to concentrate on hasty consolidation on the objective. On the hill and surrounds there were thirty enemy dead by body count.

Suddenly the skies opened up and rained mortar fire, delivered with great accuracy. We were caught in the open with nowhere to take cover and were forced to vacate the hill and beat a hasty retreat. We drew back behind the low mound of the original start line. I just made it back but not behind the rising ground as intended. I ran out of wind and simply collapsed into a shell hole. I selected this on the advice that a shell never lands in the same place twice. Catching my breath I glanced from the bottom of the shell hole at two figures near me. I saw them blown up by mortar fire and they seemed to be clutching their legs. They were the Company Commander, Maj Ben O'Dowd, and an ROK liaison officer who had just arrived on the scene.

At least we did hold the feature for about ten minutes, for the cost of two killed and fourteen wounded. One of those killed was Pte W. A. Woods, who held a DCM and MM from his service in World War II; the other was Pte R. Fisher; both were from 6 Section.

While this was going on, C Company had moved up to secure our right flank. They too came under heavy mortar fire, suffering seven wounded. One of the wounded was Cliff Nord who went on to be a Company Sergeant Major with his battalion in Malaya.

A couple of years later, in 1953, Fred Williams as a sergeant and CSM Lofty Maher and members of the then existing 2 Platoon revisited Chisan. On the hill they found great amounts of US 30 mm and 50 mm ammunition. There were also huge amounts of Gloucester Regiment uniforms, US uniforms, Chinese uniforms, stacks of steel pickets and rolls of barbed wire, all signifying varying tenancy of the real estate.

So ends Mick's account.

EIGHTEEN

ABOUT HOSPITALISATION

The treatment and evacuation system had changed dramatically since the early days of World War II. I had been wounded in the right lung before, at Derna, well up in the Libyan desert. In those days the wonder treatment was the sulpha drug. Transport of the seriously wounded was in "blood boxes", very slowly over rough, bumpy desert roads. The trip progressed by stages to a Field Ambulance unit, where we rested up, then on to the next unit, from Derna to Tobruk. I was operated on in Tobruk then went by Hospital Ship to Alexandria. All up it took two weeks. Now, in Korea, I had a shot of penicillin within hours and was admitted to a MASH that night. Not a Hot Lips Houlahan in sight, or a transvestite either, for that matter. (The Vietnam "Dust Off" system of helicopter evacuation of the wounded direct to an operating theatre within the hour is the ultimate.)

Next day I was transported by aircraft and ambulance to a US military hospital at Taegu. On arrival patients were laid out at the entrance on their stretchers where a nurse recorded details and allocated them to wards, in accordance with their injury or disease. Patients are ignored by medical staff, who discuss them as though they are inanimate blobs. My stretcher was in the charge of a big red-headed Texan orderly. The nurse could see I was not American and asked Tex where I was from. In reply he drawled, "Mam, I just ask 'em if they come from

Texas. If they don't come from Texas I don't care where they come from."

At this the nurse decided to break with tradition and consult the patient for personal details.

The casualty ward was a large marquee with about fifty beds on each side, very close together. The ward routine differed greatly from our Army Hospitals. No charts appeared to be necessary for recording medication or injections of penicillin. Everyone received the same treatment. To a timetable, tablets and other medications were issued to the entire ward, on the basis that if you didn't require it, it wouldn't harm you anyway. Similarly the staff came down the line at regular intervals, poking penicillin syringes into each of us, in turn.

(Writing about this US hospital reminds me of another I was admitted to some months later, when my knee blew up. This was a larger, more sophisticated affair with conventional wards and good facilities. One night, when the young nurse was putting the finishing touches to the ward prior to lights out, I confided to her that it was my birthday, and had I been in an Australian hospital something special would have been done for me. This pretty young thing thought for a while, then told me she did not come off duty until lights out, but would return then to give me something special. Come ten o'clock I waited in anxious anticipation. Sure enough, quiet footsteps approached the bed, guided, by a pencil of torch light. I caught the scent of her body as she leaned over me and fumbled with the buttons of my pyjama jacket. She moved her head close and whispered for me to roll over, which I did, and she rubbed my back with eau de Cologne. Then she disappeared as quietly as she had come. I thought that was sweet of her.)

At the hospital at Taegu, I was surprised to receive a visit from Major Paddy Hanway, one of our doctors and a friend from Japanese Occupation days, with whom I shared an interest in music. Paddy's job was to examine all the Australian casualties admitted this hospital, and decide whether they stayed in theatre for return to their unit, or were evacuated to Japan for further treatment in the British General Hospital in Kure.

Paddy was a character, Irish of course. He had come to Japan with the British Army but transferred to the New Zealand contingent when the Brits withdrew. With the departure of the Kiwis he switched allegiance to the Australian Army. Like all good Irishmen, Paddy enjoyed a few noggins of whiskey prior to retiring at night, and was not at his cheerful best first thing in the morning. This made it difficult for Diggers on early morning sick parade, trying to fiddle a "no duties" decision out of him. Paddy was the sickest man present; the rest were malingerers.

In Pusan Paddy lived in style, in a fine civilian house. He arranged for me to have dinner with him one night and listen to some music. He had brought his record player and an extensive collection of classical music with him. The slow movement of the Bruch G minor was disturbed by a loud banging on the front door, clearly doing nothing for Paddy's humour. And this was not improved when the banger, a US GI, requested a "prophylactic shot". Paddy did not have the faintest idea what he was talking about. This unfortunate soul then had to explain that he intended to seek out a whore, and required a shot of penicillin in case she infected him with some communicable disease. Clearly this conflicted with Paddy's medical ethics and his Irish Catholic background. He turned a dangerous colour and, losing decorum, shouted, "Get out of here you dirty bastard, and come back when you've got it."

In due course I was flown to Japan, to our General Hospital. This was a British Army establishment, conducted strictly on lines set down by Flo Nightingale. However, it was civilised enough to run to an officers' ward. The British have a cunning system to discourage patients from lingering in hospital, once anywhere near fit; they breed savage Charge Sisters. Our Officers' Ward

Matron was efficiency personified, with a vitriolic tongue. She prowled her territory like a zealous lioness, ready to pounce on the slightest infringement of her rules.

The CO was a full Colonel doctor who conducted periodic inspections. Prior to such occasions everyone who was anywhere near ambulatory was hounded into the mess room while the ward staff went diligently to work. Not a speck of dust anywhere and beds made up tight as a drum, never a wrinkle. When the inspection party was nearing the ward, we were hunted back in with threats of dire consequences should the pristine state of the ward be disturbed. Most were required to stand to attention at the foot of the bed. The really sick were permitted to sit to attention. To be allowed to lie down you had to be a candidate for the last rites.

As the great man approached each bed, the ward doctor gave him a run down on the patient. Here again one became depersonalised and was referred to as a disease or injury. "This" — pointing to me — "is a perforated thorax. I find lungs interesting. Don't you? He is also a leg."

Our dear Matron was once put to the test by a French officer who completely ignored her rules and made his own. Because he was not a British subject she did not know how to cope with him. This Frenchman was a constant source of booze. Two of his soldiers visited regularly and were given money to get him whiskey. Matron knew he had grog in the ward but could never find it. She searched lockers and delved in the cisterns in the toilet block but to no avail. It would take the indignity of a strip search to get it. The whiskey supply cut out abruptly one day, however, when the young French soldiers were caught bringing in fresh supplies and were tossed into the local slammer. (Watch your fingers. Bang!) Suggestions that he should do something to assist his unfortunate grog couriers only elicited raised eyebrows, as he applied his own logic to the situation: "I tell them to get me zee whiskey. I do not tell them to get caught."

The Frog created untold misery for Matron during one CO's inspection. He had obtained a large supply of "throw-downs", a mixture of gunpowder and flints wrapped in a small paper parcel which, when thrown on the ground or at an object, created a small explosion. After the ward had been prepared for inspection and patients were hounded back in, the Frog dashed rapidly around, scattering throw downs under the coir matting which stretched the length of each side of the ward. The entire inspection was conducted to the accompaniment of minor explosions as boots crunched on the throw-downs all the way up one side of the ward and back down the other. The Colonel and staff gave it the good old British stiff upper lip treatment, carrying on regardless. Matron, however, had fire in her eyes, and everyone knew she was having visions of someone being tied to a gun wheel and flogged.

I had a couple of brushes with this lady, and did not enjoy being eyeballed while lectured, chapter and verse, on the necessity and wisdom of the "rules".

My wounds had been relatively minor. It was the splinter in the left calf which was the main problem, giving me poor mobility for a while. However, after four weeks I was ready to go back and, conscience ridden, applied for a Movement Order to Korea, and my company.

NINETEEN

ATTACK ON "SARDINE"

I rejoined the 3rd Battalion on 14 April 1951, after a tedious trip back from Japan. I emplaned a DC3 at Iwakuni, with a group of Diggers who were returning from R & R leave in an advanced stage of having had a good time in the local canteen. In an exuberant state they gave the RAAF officer considerable trouble before settling down and buckling up. I offered my assistance but he was emphatic that I should keep right out of it and all would be well when we got in the air. Once airborne I saw clearly what he meant. The pilot bucketed the DC3 about as if in extreme turbulence, until he had a plane load of grey faces, most of them bent over spew bags. I have never seen soldiers sober up so fast.

Once in Korea I was subjected to frustrating days of shuttling from one transit unit to another, eventually arriving at 3 RAR as if by chance. In my keenness to return to my company I had cut my convalescence short and in consequence was not in very good shape. I rather expected to be spending a few days at Battalion Headquarters getting the feel of things again. However, the CO gave a friendly greeting and informed me I would be leading my company into an attack on an objective code-named Salmon, the following morning. An escort was waiting at the Signal Office to conduct me to my company.

I checked in with the Intelligence Office for a map and was briefed by our IO, Alf Argent. During April the

British Commonwealth Brigade had been engaged in Operation Rugged, attacking along parallel ridges to reach a phase line objective, Line Kansas. The crests along the ridge were code-named after fish, the last two being "Sardine" and "Salmon". One of the Middlesex companies was in the process of attacking "Sardine" that afternoon. My company was to pass through the Middlesex next morning and attack the final objective, "Salmon". This done, the area would be handed over to 6 ROK Division and the British Commonwealth Brigade could go into reserve to reorganise.

I climbed the hill to A Company with rubber legs and wheezing lungs, occasionally stopping to throw up. The Digger escorting me was patient, but I don't think I inspired visions of a dynamic company commander.

Arriving at Company Headquarters I took over from Capt Jack Gerke, who had been looking after the company in my absence. It felt good to be back with the old team again, although there had been changes. Reg Saunders was missing, having been posted as commander of C Company. My new 2iC was Captain Bob Murdoch, who proved to be a solid back-up in the difficult period we were to experience in a couple of weeks time. I was pleased to see CSM Tom Muggleton was still holding the headquarters together, and our radio operator, Lofty Heweston, was soon to go on R & R leave to Japan. Smiffy was gone and my new driver was Robert (Abdul) Guest, the son of a famous World War One RSM. Also Nunan had been medically evacuated and in his place was Bluey Mavin ("Ravin" Mavin), a very solid character to have at my side.

A message was waiting for me, informing me that the Middlesex company attack had failed, but that they would go again the following morning. I was to move A Company up behind the attacking company, ready to pass through immediately they had gained their objective, then go for "Salmon".

We had an odd experience next morning while

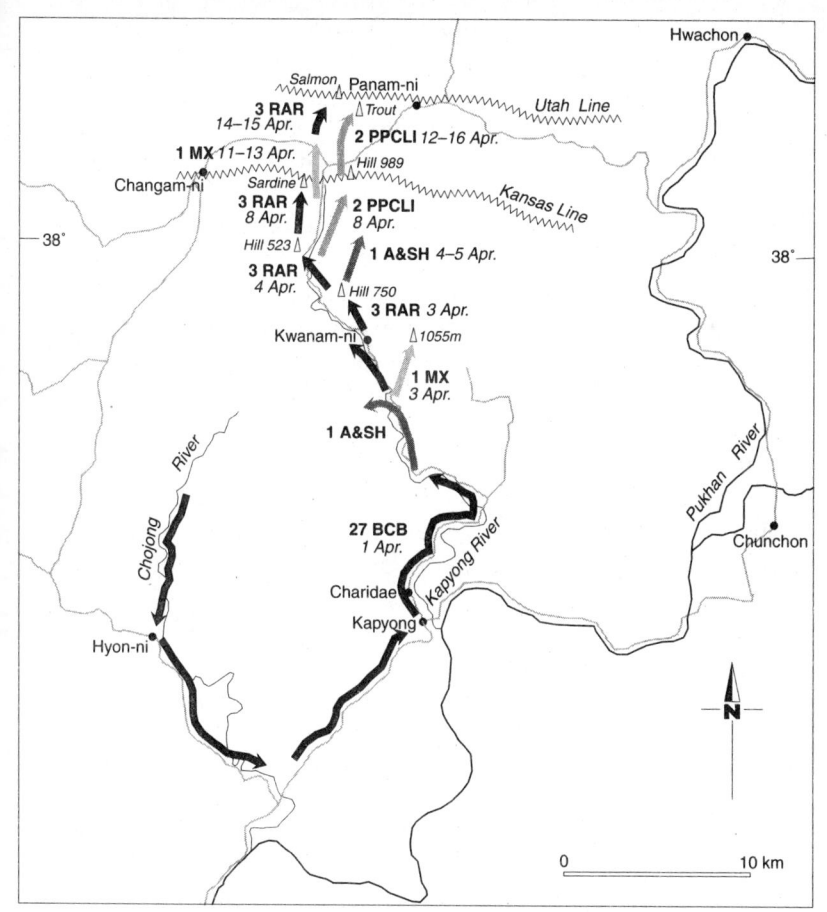

Map 13: 3 RAR movements, 1–16 April 1951

assembling the platoons in preparation for movement. The troops were in battle order, strung out on the track down the ridge. Above them, and running the length of the column, was the overhead telephone cable the signallers had strung up. As we stood there a deafening bolt of lighting struck the the cable, and flashed along it for the length of the company. Four soldiers were knocked to the ground, but on examination did not appear to be seriously harmed. They did, however, exhibit peculiar burn marks on parts of the body, similar in pattern to varicose veins. To play safe we sent them to the RAP for further examination, where Doc Beard photographed the curious burn areas for further examination at some later date.

When the company arrived at the Middlesex Regiment I checked in with the company commander who was launching the attack, and made arrangements to pass through during the consolidation phase. I settled A Company down on the reverse slope of the feature overlooking "Sardine" and joined the brigade and battalion staff officers positioned to witness the morning's proceedings.

The Middlesex had an obvious morale problem. With their battalion close to relief and a return to the good life in Hong Kong, they regarded this as a rather inappropriate time for heroics.

Their company moved to a start line in the gully below the objective and the artillery let fly with a flurry of 25-pounder shells which was not effective, worrying the Brits as much as it did the opposition, the two being in close proximity to each other. The Middlesex put in the attack but stalled. Their OC pushed them to further action but took further casualties and the attack petered out. The brigadier lost patience and told him to get his troops out of the way, saying, "Drop-kick will do it". This made me sit up, as drop-kick was a reference to the Australian Battalion, and my company was conveniently close.

Allocating me this task, Colonel Ferguson provided great incentive to succeed: "O'Dowd, the Brits have been unsuccessful twice and now all eyes are on the Australians. Don't you come back without it!"

Sardine was on a wooded ridge running east–west, parallel with the one from which we had been observing. A deep, well-timbered gully lay between. Frontal attack required descent into the gully then a rush up a sharp slope right under the enemy machine-gun and rifle fire.

This is what the Middlesex had done — twice. It was a tactic profoundly disliked by the Diggers.

The CO asked me what support I required. This was not easy to lay on. There was an abundance of 25 pounder artillery and mortar fire available, both 3 inch and 4.2, but the start line in the gully was too close to the objective to take advantage of it. I asked for the artillery and mortars to bang away to cover our movement to the start line and then cut. The MMGs were then to take over and hold the enemy heads down until I ordered "cease fire" by radio.

I gave the attack to Harold Mulry's 3 Platoon. Harold and his men required no encouragement when it came to close-quarters work. Back-up for Harold was 2 Platoon, commanded by Sgt George Harris, and I had no doubts how this team would perform. It was Freddy Gardner's 1 Platoon's turn for reserve. I instructed Harold to hit it hard and if he could take it without undue casualties to do so. If it looked too costly, he was to maintain pressure on the Chinese while Harris executed a right hook on to their left flank. And that is about the way it went.

I went with 3 Platoon to the start line in the creek where we stood aside while the Middlesex moved out with their casualties. I had the chance to exchange a few words with the disappointed Middlesex company commander, who said he thought our company would get it.

On the start line I was about to send Harold on his way when the CO called me up to enquire if I still wanted the MMGs firing on the objective. I was grateful for the remindor, for I had forgotten about them. 3 Platoon launched their attack and I followed them in. The Chinese dominated a very steep slope, from which they poured grenades and machine-gun and rifle fire. Grenades were the nuisance. They must have had an unlimited supply of these things which, fortunately, had nowhere near the killing effect of our 36 grenades. Grenades were falling everywhere around us, with the

Diggers kicking them out of the way or returning them to sender. It was clear that to rush up the incline under the enemy machine-gun and rifle fire would be costly in lives. I ordered Harold to hold and lean on the enemy, while I dispatched 2 Platoon on the prearranged right hook. 2 Platoon worked their way through the shrub to get on to the enemy flank, and engaged them. As George Harris put it:

> ... 2 Platoon moved around the outside — crossing a small creek and climbing up the spur line. Here we found a few Chinese observing the proceedings and these were dispatched promptly.[1]

From 3 Platoon position we read the enemy reaction to the threat through a slackening in the tempo of fire. I told Harold to give it another push. Never men to hesitate on such occasions, 3 Platoon charged in and got the enemy running. I don't know how far they were prepared to give chase, probably to Peking, but I ordered them to break it off and return. I got trouble over this as they wanted to go on with it, but my task was to consolidate on Sardine as a firm base for the attack on Salmon by C Company next day. The whole thing was over in about half an hour.

This action cost us eight wounded. Fortunately, nearly all the casualties were from grenades, the most serious being a soldier with a fragment in his eye and Bomber Brown's head wound. Many of the wounded men remained on duty, following a patch-up job by our medics, Nobby Clark and G. O. Cooper, or at Doc Beard's RAP.

The night passed uneventfully and next morning our clearing patrols could find no trace of the enemy on the track leading to Salmon. Later 2 Platoon opened up with Bren guns and rifles on an enemy patrol at the base of Salmon, scattering it.

Salmon was a large conical feature, wide at the bottom and tapering to the peak. With an exposed approach it offered no possibility of flanking movements. It was "up the guts" or nothing, which made me grateful I had inadvertently bought Sardine.

Next morning our company played host to the CO and his Tac HQ, plus the Brigadier and his staff, all seeking a grandstand view of the production being laid on by C Company. It was a flop. They took it without firing a shot! The luck of the draw in this game.

The following day we went happily into reserve, to enjoy a little relaxation while the 27 and 28 Brigades' changeover was effected, unaware that our next fixture was less than two weeks away — the Battle of Kapyong.

TWENTY
PLAN AUDACIOUS

On 23 April 1951 the 27th British Commonwealth Brigade was pitchforked into a battle without any warning. During April 1951 the Brigade Headquarters with its two British battalions was in the process of packing up for return to garrison duties in Hong Kong. The Argylls were already in Pusan boarding ship, and brigade HQ and Middlesex were preparing to follow them. The 28th British Brigade with its Kings Shropshire Light Infantry (KSLI) and Kings Own Scottish Borderers (KOSB) was preparing to come forward to absorb 3 RAR, Princess Patricia's Canadian Light Infantry, the NZ 16 Artillery Regiment and the Indian Field Ambulance to create the new 28th British Commonwealth Brigade. In this state of flux we believed it was impossible that we could be committed to operations. Corps HQ must also have considered 27 BCB to be off the order of battle, for they did not find it necessary to brief the brigadier on Plan Audacious.

Appendix A is a paper produced from research into this plan by Jack Gallaway. It is fully authenticated with footnotes providing references for those wishing to study the subject further. This chapter is an encapsulated version of the plan, and its fate when tested on the enemy.

Chinese soldiers were not trained to refuse to divulge tactical information when taken prisoner. In consequence, they gave quite frank responses to questioning, sometimes exhibiting pride in what their masters were preparing to do to the UN Force. Information obtained from prisoners in March and April and supported by air reconnaissance and other intelligence sources confirmed beyond doubt that the Chinese were in the process of preparing for a major attack. All prisoners agreed that it would be launched about 22 April. Gen Ridgway saw in this an opportunity to inflict a devastating defeat on the enemy, and drew up Plan Audacious accordingly.

The two well-worn invasion routes for the capture of Seoul were (1) along the west coast on the Imjim River and (2) down the Kapyong Valley. Ridgway's plan called for a strengthening of the whole of Line Kansas north of Seoul, except for the Kapyong Valley approach. To prevent an enemy break-through at the Imjim, he positioned some of his best formations there, including three US divisions, the Turk Brigade and the British 29 Brigade Group with its Centurion tanks. Formations in that area were those which could be relied upon to fight and hold ground. In the centre the Kapyong Valley mouth was sixteen kilometres wide. On the left of it Ridgway put the 24 US Division with orders to hold. On the right of the valley the battle-hardened US Marine Division took up position, also with orders to hold. The sixteen kilometres between these divisions was loosely held by the 6 ROK Division.

Sitting in reserve near Seoul lay the 1st Cavalry Division, with its three Regimental Combat Teams ready to burst on the scene at the critical moment.

Ridgway well knew that 6 ROK Division held the course record for putting distance between itself and the Chinese, on first contact. Relying on this he invited the enemy to surge down the Kapyong Valley as the ROKs gave ground, 24 US Division and the Marines holding firm on the flanks. With the enemy sucked into the Valley, the Cavalry Division was to charge across to link up with 24 Division and the Marines, thus trapping large numbers of Chinese in the Kapyong Valley salient, cut

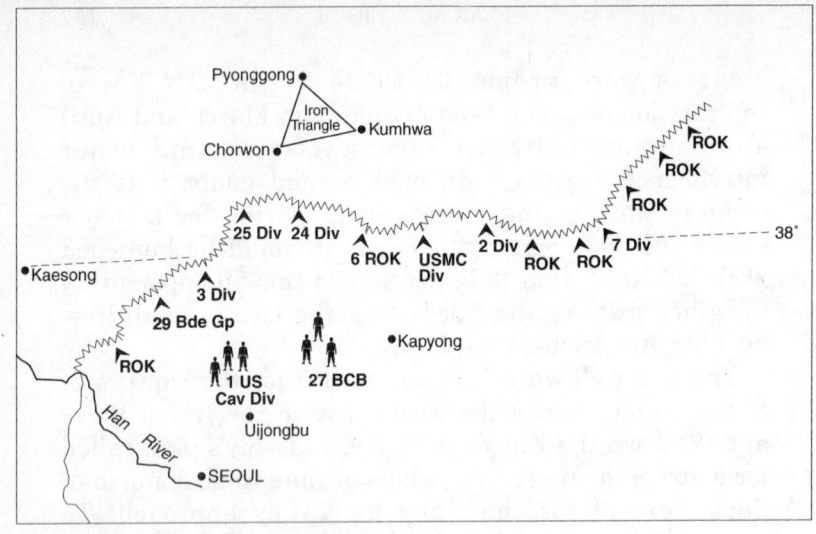

Map 14: The Kansas Line, 22 April 1951

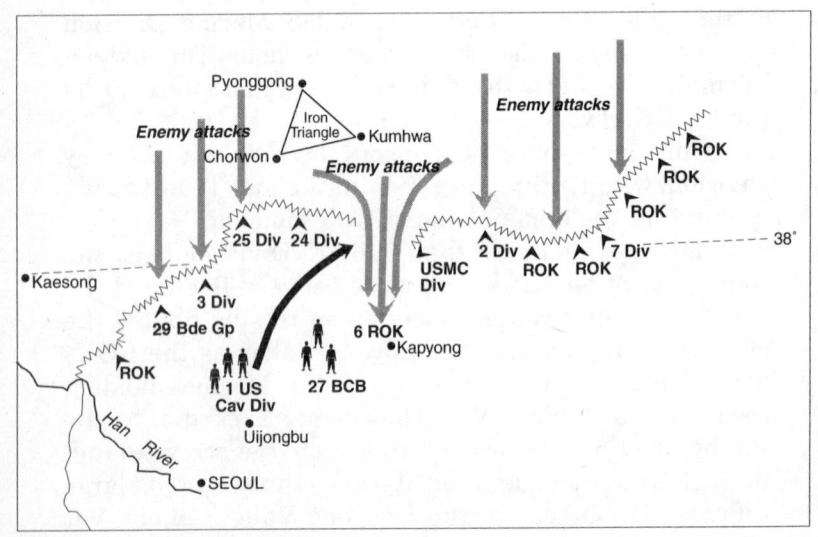

Map 15: Proposed plan "Audacious"

off from their lines of communication and supply. (See Maps 14 and 15.)

The 27th British Commonwealth Brigade had no role in this manoeuvre, and consequently was not briefed about it.

The generals smiled on Audacious, regarding it as a winner. However, they were not listening to old Helmut von Moltke, who warned us that no plan survives first contact with the enemy. After Audacious he could have been forgiven for rising from the grave to say, "Told you so!"

The Chinese launched their attack dead on time, hammering at defences on the west flank at the Imjim, pushing the British 29th Brigade back, capturing the Gloucesters and making inroads elsewhere and offering a serious threat to Seoul. The situation deteriorated so rapidly that two regiments of the Cavalry Division had to be committed to stem the flood. Thus the reserve at Seoul was reduced to just one regiment, leaving no possibility of closing the gap between 24 Division and the Marines. Audacious was as dead as the dodo!

At this time the only part of Audacious still functioning according to plan was the Chinese Army streaming down the Kapyong Valley, on its way to capture Seoul. Out of sheer desperation the totally unprepared 27 BCB was dumped in the path of the enemy's thrust, with the Diggers of 3 RAR stuck out in front to take the initial impact.

TWENTY-ONE

THE BATTLE OF KAPYONG

On reserve the battalion was enjoying some respite from operations, bivouacked in a pleasant wooded area not far from the town of Kapyong, blissfully unaware of the threat imposed by Plan Audacious. We were on fresh rations, which the soldiers had not experienced for some time, a steady issue of beer was available and the tranquillity and warmth of early spring created a relaxed, holiday ambience. Soon we were to celebrate Anzac Day with the 16th New Zealand Artillery Regiment and the Turkish Brigade — all the original cast represented on another battlefield. We planned a short parade, followed by a rerun of the Gallipoli battle, using stubbies for ammunition.

We took advantage of the lull in proceedings to dispatch some men on R & R leave, including two key members: my command net radio operator, Lofty Heweston, and CSM Muggleton. This probably saved Lofty's life, for it was to cost his replacement, Harry Bolitho, his.

On the morning of the 23rd I lay stretched out on the grass enjoying a carefree doze when Harry Bolitho shattered my dreams with an urgent message: companies were on half an hour's notice to move and the Orders Group was to assemble at the village of Chuktun-ni. I instructed Bob Murdoch to prepare the troops, check out the F Echelon vehicles and stores, and stand by.

At Chuktun-ni we were briefed by the CO that the 6

ROK Division held the front about eighteen kilometres north of our position; they were under attack but holding. We were to conduct reconnaissance to lay out a blocking position to be occupied later, should this become necessary. Once this was done we could return to the battalion area and get on with our relaxation. Since the orders were delivered on a small feature just forward of the 6 ROK Divisional Headquarters, there seemed to be no great urgency in the situation.

The CO had been badly misled. Long before this briefing took place, 6 ROK Division had broken. While we breakfasted that morning, thousands of ROK soldiers were fleeing towards us, hotly pursued by the Communist Chinese Forces. The NZ Artillery Regiment supporting this ROK Division had earlier reported ROK soldiers streaming through their gun lines, but the message did not get through to brigade headquarters, leaving us ignorant of the urgency of the situation.

It is difficult to understand why our masters didn't expect this to be the immediate consequence of an enemy attack on any ROK Division, or, more importantly, why those in charge of our immediate destiny, our CO and Brigadier, had not been properly briefed on the danger. We had seen how 6 ROK Division had broken and run at Tokchon on New Year's Day, opening the way for the capture of Seoul.

By necessity the brigade was to be deployed over an extremely wide area, with frightening gaps between units. In turn, the battalion had to accept an extended front with consequential gaps between sub-units. The intended brigade disposition called for two battalions forward on dominating features each side of the Kapyong Road, 3 RAR on the right from the road to Hill 504, the Middlesex Regiment left (west) of 3 RAR on the mountain, Sudok San. The Princess Pats were to be positioned south of 1 Middlesex on Hill 677, guarding a road leading in from the north-west. The 16th NZ Field

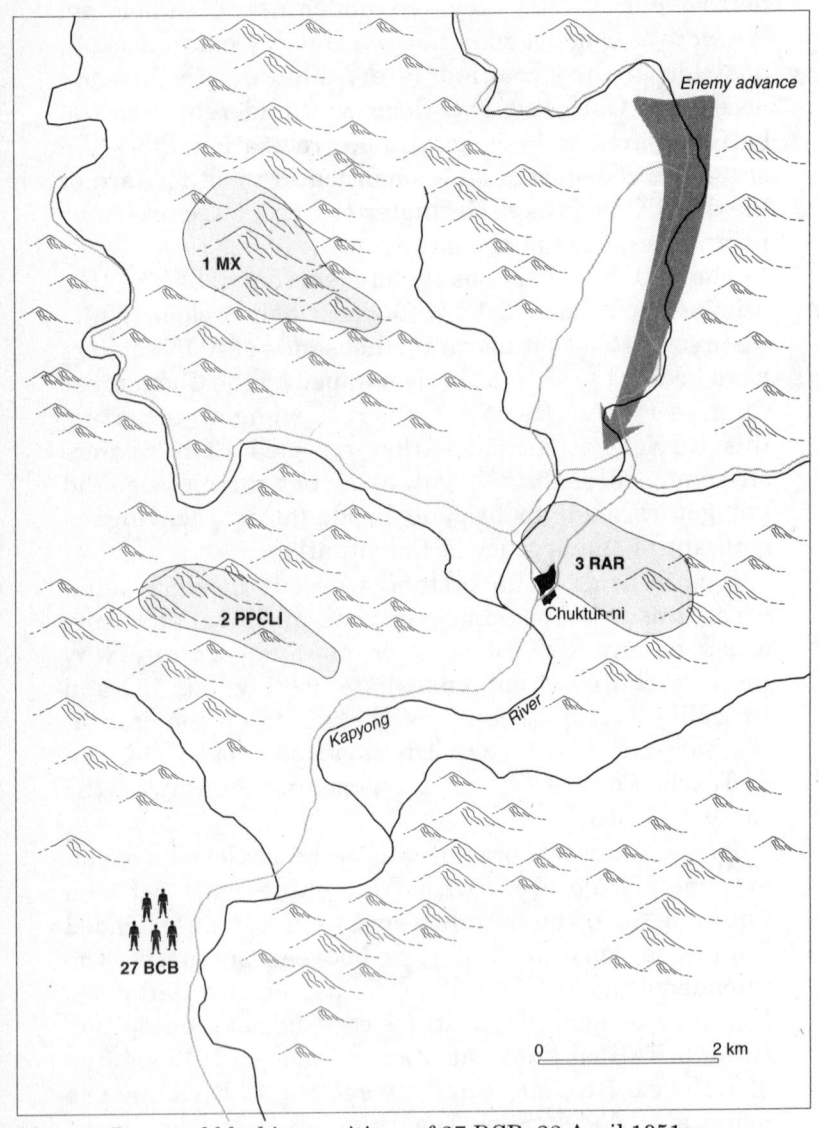

Map 16: Proposed blocking positions of 27 BCB, 23 April 1951

Regiment was to be located rear of the Canadians. (See Map 16.)

Unsatisfactory as this deployment was, it became even worse. The Field Regiment (less one battery) was ordered forward to support 6 ROK Division. However, the ability of the ROKs to keep the enemy away from the guns was suspect, so the Middlesex was dispatched to provide cover for them. It transpired that neither of these units returned in time to take up their battle positions. With the Middlesex not in occupation of Sudok San, 3 RAR's rifle companies were stuck out on their own, and with the guns not surveyed in, A Company was fated to fight a major night battle without close artillery support. (See Map 17.)

While the Orders Group was still in progress, the order came through for the position to be occupied. Discarding happy anticipation of the pleasures back at the bivouac we went to work on reconnaissance, in preparation for the arrival of the companies.

The battalion was deployed with B, A and D companies forward and C in reserve. Battalion HQ and the Support Company platoons were about 1300 metres to the rear.

B Company, commanded by Capt Darcy Laughlin, was on the left, responsible for the road and located on a low feature running parallel to it. On a small knoll forward of the company Laughlin established a standing patrol commanded by Cpl Clem Kealy.

A Company was across the road from B Company on a spur which climbed steadily from the valley floor to the 504-metre peak where Norm Gravener's D Company, occupied the vital ground. About halfway down the ridge from D Company a secondary spur forked off to the south-west, forming a re-entrant between it and A Company. On this fork C Company, now commanded by Capt Reg Saunders, was in reserve.

A Company's responsibility, extending from the road to D Company, was far too much territory for one company, two would have had difficulty in covering it.

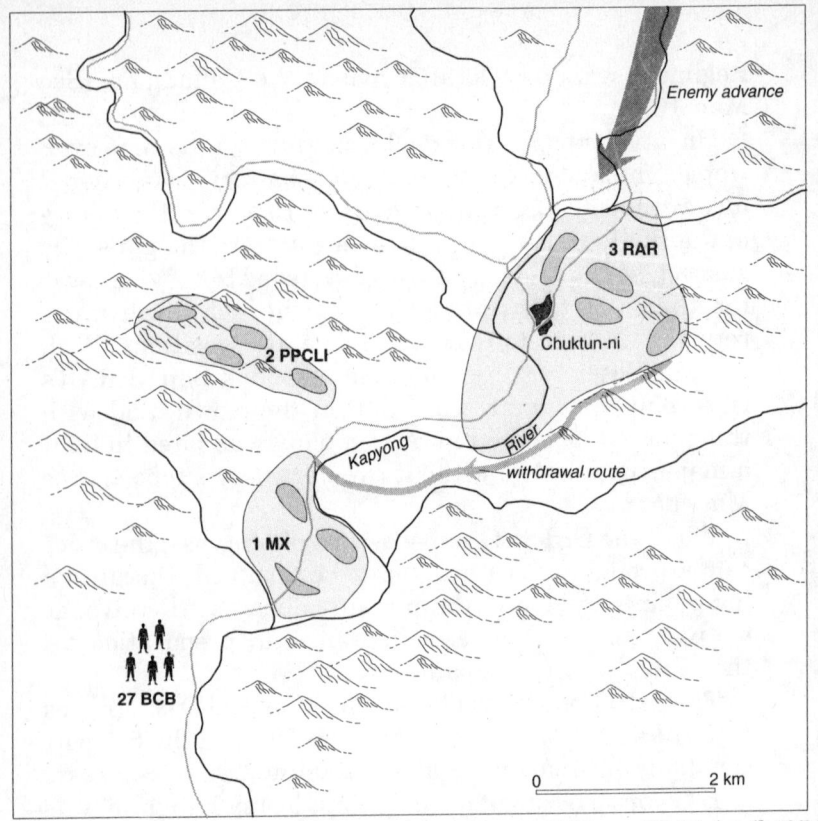

Map 17: Actual blocking positions occupied by 27 BCB, on 23–24 April 1951 and 3 RAR withdrawal route

At the Orders Group I had requested an extra platoon, Anti-Tank or Assault Pioneer, but this was refused. Instead Sgt Lennie Lenoy's Medium Machine Gun Section was allocated to provide some additional manpower. For me it was a classic case of "occupy the lot and be weak everywhere, or concentrate at a defendable point". Having a responsibility to support B Company in denying the road to the enemy, I concentrated the company opposite the road on the lower end of our ridge. This left a tremendous gap between A and D companies for which absolutely nothing could have been done beyond registration of artillery defensive fire tasks, but in the circumstances such support was denied me.

The lower end of our spur was reasonably level for about 100 metres and accommodated 1 and 3 Platoons, Company HQ and the Medium Machine Gun Section. The ground then rose sharply to a knoll overlooking 1 and 3 Platoons and here I established 2 Platoon to provide cover for the main position below it. The unoccupied rising ground between 3 and 2 Platoons was a problem, but without additional troops nothing could be done about it. (See Map 18.)

The US 72nd Heavy Tank Battalion (Shermans[1]) provided a Tank Company of three platoons, each of five tanks, commanded by Lt Kenneth W. Koch. An odd relationship existed between the tanks and 3 RAR. They were neither under command nor in support, merely in location. Koch operated completely independently of CO 3RAR or anyone else. Any direct assistance provided was either in response to a cry for help or unexpected involvement in our tactical situations at the tank commanders' initiative. In the days prior to occupation of the blocking position, Koch had flown the area on reconnaissance. (This smelt of the planning for Audacious.)[2]

For the night of the 23rd one tank platoon was located forward of B Company where the road crossed the ford,

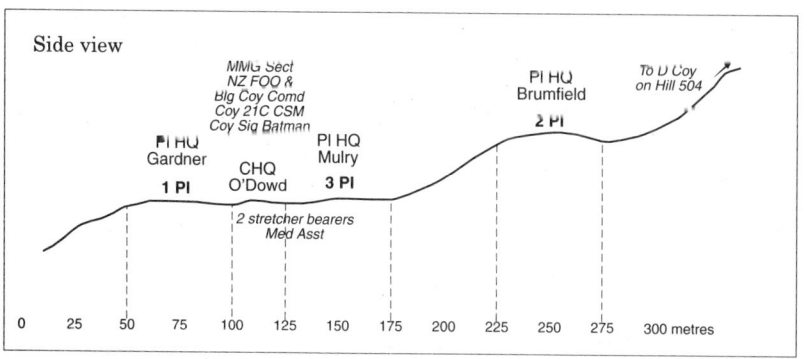

Map 18: Layout of A Company positions, 1900 hrs, 23–24 April 1951

one on the road opposite C Company and the other back at Battalion Headquarters. These platoons were positioned by Koch without consultation with Darcy Laughlin or me, or, as far as I know, Lt Col Ferguson. He was his own boy, ignoring considerations of tank infantry mutual support or cooperation.

Long before our deployment the Chinese had broken the ROK Division defences and were well on their way towards us. The NZ Field Regiment War Diary records that the forward battery observers reported at 0300 hours on the 23rd, that ROK stragglers were swarming past their guns, but we were oblivious to this threatening situation.[3]

An ROK Divisional Commander has his hand held by a US Army full Colonel from the Korean Military Advisory Group, whose duty was to influence the Divisional Commander's decision making.[4] The CO positioned our Intelligence Sergeant, Colin McGregor, in the ROK Division HQ with the idea of providing early warning of ROK nervousness. Colin described the situation in the headquarters:

> The ROK Headquarters consisted of the GOC, a few staff officers and an American Korean Military Advisory Group colonel plus miscellaneous troops ... As I watched, the map staff continually moved the positions of friendly troops further south and replaced them with red arrows showing the Chinese Communist Force advance ... my last glimpse of the situation map showed two brigades were approximately six miles north of the battalion position.[5]

Our 2iC, Bob Murdoch, brought the company forward and it was quickly put on the ground. On the left and nearest the road 1 Platoon took up defence. I put the Medium Machine Gun Section and Company HQ personnel between 1 Platoon and 3 Platoon which covered the remainder of the lower or main position. On the knoll overlooking our main position I located 2 Platoon, giving away the intervening ground. Their commander, Lt Lou Brumfield, was a graduate of the Royal Military College who had joined the company only a few days previously. This was to be his introduction to fighting but he proved to have a cool head and took the situation in his stride.[6]

Sergeant George Harris was acting Sergeant Major, responsible for headquarters personnel and ammunition supply. I had used George in various capacities and he always served me well, and Kapyong was to be no exception. CSM Tom Muggleton had returned from R & R leave in Japan but could not get past Battalion HQ in time to join us. Like the gentlemen abed in England, he cursed sitting this one out on the interchange bench.

Occupation of a defensive position had developed into a routine process during the fluid operations of the past eight months. We had dug defences all over North and South Korea and by now section commanders had only to be allocated tasks and they would proceed with little need for supervision. They knew what was required and, more to the point, knew the penalty for getting it wrong. However, the ground was not kind, being still part frozen from the vicious Korean winter. It was hard digging and in places there was rock just below the surface, or outcropping.

A hot evening meal was provided. Having only fresh rations, the Quarter Master Sergeant, S/Sgt Bill Mann, was unable to issue the troops with the usual twenty-four hour combat ration pack, and apparently unit administration was not up to delivering them to us from the B Echelon stores vehicles. In consequence, this was our last food or drink until the operation was over. The meal disposed of, Bob Murdoch unloaded our reserve ammunition, cleared the decks of surplus items and dispatched our vehicles to the rear.

Dusk saw the first indications that things had gone wrong when a noisy stream of ROK soldiers began making a hasty exit south, down the road between B Company and us. No cause for panic yet. Soon, however, we had good reason to take another look at defence preparations, as this stream developed into a panic-ridden, unruly mob, running and shouting in terror, as though the very devil was on their heels, as well he may have been. A really ominous situation developed when civilian refugees began to appear, intermingled with the stream of ROK soldiers. Women, old men and crying children were carrying their meagre possessions on their backs, and some were leading animals. It was a pitiful sight — a frightened population fleeing before a hated enemy. From past experience we knew that, come dusk, the Chinese would mix in with the refugees, and ROK soldiers for that matter, and use them as cover to infiltrate to our rear.

The road was B Company's responsibility, so I called up Darcy Laughlin, suggesting he put out a section to filter the mob and ascertain when the Chinese began to enter the area, at which time I could very effectively clear the road with Lenny Lenoy's Medium Machine Guns.[7] Obviously Darcy did not share my concern. As dark settled in I rang the CO and requested permission to open fire with Lenoy's machine-guns, to stop all movement on the road. This was refused on the grounds that I had no identified enemy and ROK soldiers could still be coming through. I wore this until the odd shot rang out then repeated my request. This prompted the accusation, "O'Dowd, you are panicking". Well, he got that right! Nevertheless, little satisfaction was derived when the panic became justified as firing broke out to the rear of us among the Support Company platoons shielding Battalion Headquarters. We now had confirmation that the enemy was at our rear, isolating the rifle companies from the rest of the battalion. Undoubtedly we would be attacked just as soon as the enemy was organised for it.

Hostilities opened forward of B Company just after dark, with the US tank platoon at the ford. Without infantry cover for the tanks the Chinese were able to get among them and it was fortunate they did not possess anti-tank weapons.

With poor night vision the tank commanders had to direct fire from the open turret position, and predictably the Chinese shot them. The tanks then closed down and the enemy got into the spirit of things, clambering all over them, searching for opportunities to pop in a burst of small-arms fire or damage tracks. To counter this, the Sherman crews resorted to hosing each other down with machine-gun fire and rotating the turrets to knock the enemy off. Eventually the tanks withdrew, having accomplished precisely nothing.

Complete disregard for the principals of infantry–tank cooperation had been demonstrated by both arms. Devastating effect could have been achieved with the tremendous firepower of those five tanks properly sited in conjunction with infantry. There is a lesson there somewhere.

With the tanks departed from the scene the enemy continued probing forward towards B Company, causing Cpl Kealy's outpost patrol to return to 4 Platoon. The enemy located B Company and instigated a fire fight which Murdoch and I followed with great interest, in the hope that Darcy would keep the Chinese entertained for the remainder of the night. It was not to be. The situation quietened down over the road and soon we became aware of the presence of the enemy milling around somewhere in the valley below us, making preparations for attack. The main event was about to get under way.

An entry in the 27th Brigade War Diary for 23 April notes a request for defensive fire at about midnight, but fails to explain who it came from, or why such a request should be made to brigade HQ instead of the artillery. The following Diary entry notes the departure of 16 Field Artillery Regiment to a new position, in rear of Brigade HQ. There is no record in either War Diary that the request was passed to the Kiwi Gunners, or that it was acted upon.

It would have been comforting to have artillery registered at this time so that defensive fire tasks could smash up the enemy in their assembly areas. But there was a problem with the guns. They had been forward supporting the 6 ROK Division, protected by the Middlesex. These units returned to brigade after dark and were unable to take up battle positions. I had an artillery Forward Observation Officer, Lt Dennis Fielden, and requested him to register his guns for tasks in areas where I considered enemy threats might develop. Dennis informed me that he could not provide any support because the guns had moved into position after dark, and were not surveyed in. I have to believe this, because Dennis was killed during the night and both his radio operators, Gunners Kemp and Mulligan, were wounded, one of them fatally, when effective artillery support might have saved their lives.

Royal Australian Artillery officers I have since consulted on this matter cannot understand why Fielden did not put a round down at a safe distance and correct by carefully decreasing range. He was not very experienced as an artillery Forward Observation Officer.

Some years later Darcy Laughlin, describing the B Company action on the night of the 23–24 April, stated that he had had artillery close support. I could not understand how he could have obtained this while it had been denied to me. Evidence from subsequent investigation proved that close artillery support for B Company was not possible during the night of 23–24 April.

Darcy's NZ Field Regiment FOO, Lt Don Scott, states categorically that he did not register his guns, and was never requested to do so. Furthermore, he was not in communication with either his guns or the Battery Commander, Maj Buzz Hunt, during the night. This is supported by the Battery Commander's radio operator, Gnr Colin Luskie,[8] who stated that his radio was not employed for fire control during the night.

In correspondence Ian McGibbon, a New Zealand historian, suggested that Laughlin could have registered the guns himself, using Line Observer Target procedure. Quite apart from the flawed logic of Darcy conducting registration himself when he had a Kiwi gunner officer available to do this for him, it would have required Darcy and his radio operator, Kevin Hatfield, to locate themselves forward to call fall of shot. Hatfield, in a tape-recorded interview available in 3 RAR museum, is adamant that the company communications were not used for such purposes, and that Laughlin did not leave his Command Post during the night.[9]

The commander of the standing patrol forward of B Company, Cpl Clem Kealy,[10] would have been painfully aware of shells exploding in front of him, and in a taped interview available in 3 RAR Museum he denies this happening. Additionally, the tank platoon forward of Kealy's patrol would not have enjoyed or forgotten the experience of shells bursting in their vicinity, and there is no mention of it in their "After Action Report".[11]

During my army career I had been subjected to artillery fire at Bardia, Tobruk and Derna and in New Guinea. We had used both US 105 mm and NZ 25-pounder guns previously in Korea. I was well experienced at recognising incoming and outgoing artillery fire, and I know we had no such support on the first night of Kapyong. Furthermore, I cannot find another soldier who experienced it that night.

Kiwi gunners always supported 3 RAR willingly and well, but for whatever reason we received no support during the night of 23–24 April 1951. I understand they fired a tremendous number of shells that night, but these must have been in support of the Canadians or somewhere well out of hearing from our location.

I also had US 4.2 inch and 3 RAR mortar mobile fire controllers who were similarly handicapped. By the time the US 4.2 mortar fire controller joined me, shooting had broken out in the rear and his gun crews had taken to the hills, leaving their mortars and vehicles behind. However the US fire control officer took up a rifle and went to work with the rest. My 3 inch mortar fire controller, Ron Perkins, had a problem too. Back at the base-plate position the Mortar Platoon commander, Capt Phil Bennett, and his mortar crews were at that time very busily employed fighting the Chinese off.[12]

The impending battle was to be a very personal affair. In addition to a lack of fire support of any sort, we had no wire, no anti-personnel mines, or any other impediment to interpose between attacker and defender. It was to be soldier against soldier at very close range in the dark. There was absolutely nothing I could do to help my men, beyond walking up and down, watching for the possibility of a break-in, and shouting encouragement while attacks were in progress.

The A Company battle started with the usual gambit — probing patrols bumping the forward weapon pits, feeling for soft spots, and the Diggers shooting them back into the dark. When the enemy had had enough of this, they resorted to their standard attack routine which was repeated for the remainder of the night:

- From somewhere down in the gully below us a discordant flurry of bugles and whistles would be heard, as the commanders assembled their soldiers and organised them for the attack.
- Then there was silence, as they crept up the hill towards us.
- Next came a hail of hand grenades, intended to put the defenders' heads down.
- Finally there was the assault, launched with determination and ferocity, wave upon wave.

All hell broke loose as the Diggers cut down the surge of attackers, pouring into them as much rapid fire as their weapons could produce, the Owen sub-machine-gun being the most effective for this, and the dear old single-shot Lee Enfield rifle the least. To prevent being overrun, all killing had to be effected in the brief exposure from when the enemy became dimly visible from out of

THE BATTLE OF KAPYONG

the dark until they reached the forward weapon pits — a killing field of fire from about five metres to zero. 3 Platoon fired off a few 2 inch mortar illuminating flares, but I quickly put a stop to this because they completely destroyed night vision. When the Diggers had slaughtered enough of the attackers, the enemy pulled back, giving a short respite from the fighting. In this period the platoon and section commanders furiously went about removing their dead and wounded to the reverse slope of the main position. Here Bob Murdoch accounted for the casualties while the RAAMC Medical Orderly, Cpl Nobby Clark, and his stretcher-bearers worked on the wounded.

The commanders then rapidly redeployed their men so that each forward weapon pit was occupied by at least one fit man. Then these magnificent soldiers steadied themselves to meet the next onslaught. No sooner would reorganisation be complete than the discordant orchestra below would start up again, heralding the next attack. 1 Platoon, being closest to the road, received a lot of attention on its left flank in addition to the front. They put up a magnificent fight, the Platoon Sergeant, Vic Svenson, and another soldier going through a number of cases of 36 grenades to break up the attacks. Nevertheless, 1 Platoon took very heavy casualties until eventually Fred Gardiner had to inform me he did not have enough men left to stand off another assault. With considerable reluctance I relinquished the lower end of the ridge to the enemy and brought what was left of 1 Platoon in alongside the MMG Section and 3 Platoon and arranged them to confront the recently vacated ground. Predictably the Chinese occupied the vacated 1 Platoon area with their next attack, and held it for the remainder of the night.

I now had the ludicrous situation of three platoons on the feature, one of them being Chinese and definitely not under command. This situation was precarious to say the least. Through attrition the forward pits were now very sparsely manned. Had the enemy on our left attacked that flank in conjunction with a frontal attack we may well have been in more trouble than we could handle. I waited in dread of this but, inexplicably, the occupants of Freddie's previous position did not attack. I could only surmise that they did not have an officer, or some person with authority, to organise them.

It was at about this time that I got the bad news that the MMG Section Commander, Sgt Lennie Lenoy, had been killed. Lennie went a long way back in 3 RAR Occupation days. He was a great soldier. well respected and liked by everyone. It was also a bad night for Signal Platoon attachments, as Harry Bolitho and Bernie Goldsmith were killed and Arthur Prior wounded. "Ossie" Osbaldistone then took over as operator of the company radio on the command net.

One can only conjecture about enemy casualties, but they must have been tremendous, for they poured themselves into the defenders' fire. From 0200 or 0300 hours the attacks became sporadic and less savage, leading us to deduce that enough of the enemy had been killed to take the sting out of the force confronting us. However, life was not made any more pleasant when they ranged in on us with mortars firing high-explosive and incendiary bombs. The incendiaries set a low heather fire running through the defence, with a thick blanket of smoke and exploding ammunition adding to the distress of the casualties.

Throughout the night I had been apprehensive about the gap in the rising ground between 3 Platoon and 2 Platoon. (See Map 18.) A perilous situation would develop if the enemy occupied it; 2 Platoon would be cut off and our main position dominated. Just prior to dawn it happened, an enemy machine-gun crew got established there and proceeded to make life very uncomfortable by directing fire into us. More to the point their commander maintained repeated blasts on his whistle, drawing attention to his discovery, no doubt pleading for reinforcement. I judged them to be immediately below 2 Platoon and directed Lou Brumfield to lay on searching fire to flush them out. This he did with enthusiasm, with some of the rounds landing on our position. I ordered this firing to cease and told Lou to organise a fighting patrol to clean them out. He sent the acting platoon sergeant, Cpl Jim Everleigh, with Cpl Bill Sinclair's 6 Section. They located the machine-gun crew and charged into them with a neat action, wiping them out. However, it was not without cost. On arrival at my headquarters Everleigh reported that Private Bill (Sailor) Jillet had been lightly wounded, but shortly after I was informed that this good soldier had died of his wounds.

It was now dawn and, with the enemy machine-gun nest silenced, most firing had ceased. However, at about this time another soldier was killed. Vic Carr reports:

> Dawn had broken, fire had slackened due to 2 Pl's section attack on the gun position, and Allen (Rimmer) and I were congratulating each other on having survived another action, when a single round was fired and it struck the edge of the pit and showered us with dirt, and the round then hit Allen in the cheek, killing him instantly.

I was now able to direct my attention to the uncomfortable situation of the Chinese troops occupying 1 Platoon's ground. Once again I had to call on Harold Mulry's 3 Platoon to restore the situation. I instructed him to organise his men to counter-attack and drive the enemy from our ridge.

Without fuss Mulry selected a group of his troops and quickly arranged them in attack formation. Harris and some others joined in uninvited. The Diggers were in a pretty savage mood by now and charged in through the undergrowth, yelling and firing from the hip. The Chinese had by far the superiority in numbers but surprise was an important ingredient in the attack. The shock of having this bunch of madmen ripping into them sent this unfortunate bunch fleeing in the direction of the road. As far as ground was concerned we had restored the status quo, but we did not have the numbers to occupy it all.

On recovering 1 Platoon's position, we were surprised to discover that one of our wounded had been overlooked in the dark the previous night, when Freddie's men withdrew, and he had been taken prisoner by the Chinese. He told us that when Harold's men came charging in the Chinese soldiers pushed him into a weapon pit where he would be sheltered from our fire. This was a side of the enemy we had not expected.

It was at this time that firing broke out all over our front and on investigation I discovered the Diggers having a great time with a shooting gallery in the paddy fields forward of us. Daylight had caught the enemy out in the open, behind tufts of heather, folds in the ground and so on. Every time one or a group made a dash for more secure cover the game was on. I won no popularity points for ordering platoon commanders to put a stop to it. We had used a lot of ammunition during the night, resupply was by no means assured, and development of the tactical situation from here left no room for optimism.

During the night A Company took heavy casualties. Normally Battalion Headquarters would have provided jeep ambulances to evacuate the wounded to the RAP for treatment and movements to the Field Ambulance. However, with the enemy operating in rear of the rifle companies, evacuation was not possible. Nobby Clark and his bearers did everything possible to care for the wounded but the meagre resources of their medical bags were not designed for the situation that confronted them. Having only two stretchers meant that most of the wounded had to be laid out on the frozen ground, exposed to the cold all night. Although every effort was made to cover them, it was impossible to keep them warm.

Nobby had no means of treating shock, no way of alleviating pain. Some who died would have survived had it been possible to evacuate them to the Field Ambulance unit. Some could have hung on if it had been possible to keep them warm. Casualty treatment was a very unhappy aspect at Kapyong, but all that could be done to save life and relieve suffering was done. I trust that a more enlightened approach has been taken towards this sort of problem for the company medical staff of a modern infantry battalion.

From daylight the battle shifted to D Company and Norman Gravener and I maintained contact. D Company held the vital ground above us. If we lost that, the rifle companies below would fall like apples on the end of a branch. To compensate for the lack of air or artillery the Chinese normally chose to attack under cover of darkness. However, the tactical importance of Hill 504 was such that they attempted to take it in daylight. The first enemy probing came in on Lt Ward's 12 Platoon at about 0400 when a small party hit them. One of the enemy was killed and one taken prisoner. At 0700 hours 12 Platoon was attacked by an enemy force employing grenades, mortars and small arms. This force was restricted by the narrow ridge, which enabled 12 Platoon to deal with it savagely. 12 Platoon was attacked every half hour until 1000 hours and then sporadically for the remainder of the day, but platoon small-arms fire and artillery barrages kept the enemy at bay.

The narrow east–west configuration of A Company ground dictated linear defence, but D Company's ground projected south–north toward the enemy, forcing him to employ a lay-back, reverse-slope position, platoons one behind the other. (See Map 19.) Norman did not have an artillery fire controller but he was a very experienced officer, having served in the Middle East, New Guinea and with the British Army in Burma prior to enlisting for Korea. By daylight the 16th NZ Field Artillery Regiment was on line again, so he was able to very effectively register targets employing Line Observer Target procedure. He laid down 25-pounder shell fire in front of 12 Platoon and adjusted from there for the remainder of the day. Every enemy attack was met with

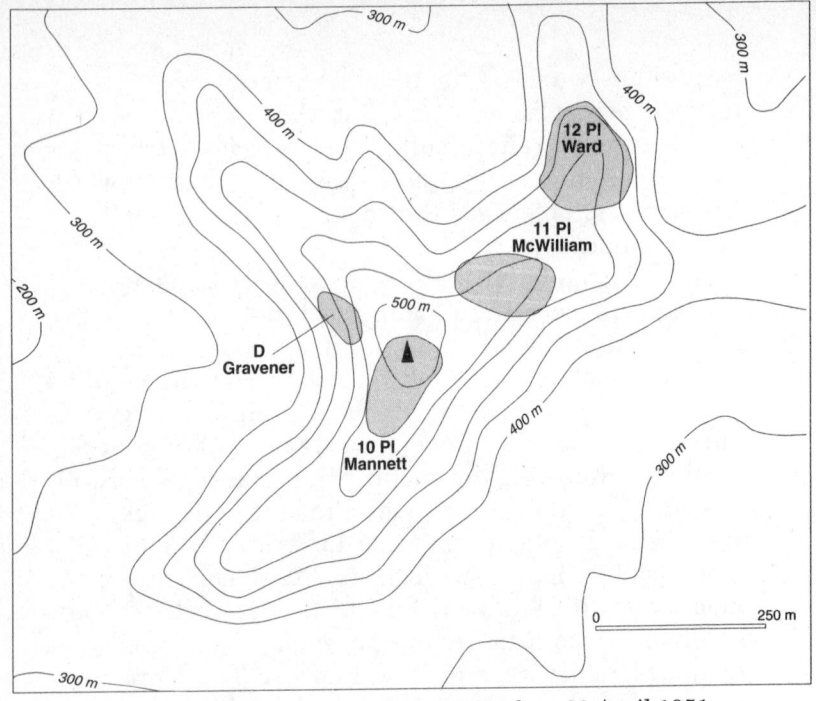

Map 19: Layout of D Company positions, 1900 hrs, 23 April 1951

a devastating 25-pounder barrage and effective, aggressive defence from the platoon's small arms. The reports I got from Norman were that they had the situation under control.

With D Company holding firm and the eviction of our overnight lodgers I now had time, for the first time in twelve hours, to consider matters other than what was going on immediately around me. I had not had communication from the CO all night, and wondered what the situation was like behind us. He did not make contact with the rifle companies until after daylight on the 24th.[13] The telephone line from Battalion HQ to B Company was in operation all night. Telephone cable had been laid down the west side of the road to B Company and from there across the road to A, C and D companies. Since two platoons of Sherman tanks used the road both to get into position and then later to withdraw, lines across the road had a brief life. The command radio net should have become the prime means of communication between CO and company commanders as soon as the telephone line went out, but according to the CO's radio operator, Cpl Lindsay Beeck, this means was never activated.[14] When the CO departed for the Middlesex area at about midnight,[15] he did not take his radio operator with him. In any event, the telephone line remained operative to B Company all night. Had anyone at Battalion HQ been curious about the rifle company's problems we could have been contacted by radio or relay through B Company.[16]

My meditations were interrupted by advice that the CO had been on air to B Company and given them approval to cross the road to join C Company in reserve behind me. I reacted sharply to this, because enemy occupation of their feature surrendered control of the road, and exposed my left flank. From his location with the Middlesex, some four kilometres or so to the rear, the CO was in no position to appreciate the tactical consequences of this decision. I called him immediately and insisted B Company should remain. He ignored this and requested a report on the local situation, which I supplied. I requested urgent resupply of essential items. He said he would see what could be done, then reminded me that I was the senior rifle company commander, a reference to the Standing Operating Procedure whereby the senior company commander automatically assumed command when the CO was not in a position to exercise tactical control of the rifle companies. Throughout the day I maintained contact with the other rifle company commanders, particularly D Company, but the CO did not officially hand over command until the time for withdrawal was authorised.

During B Company's movement across the road two events occurred worth reporting. This company had taken no casualties at all during the night, but got their first during the crossing, when Private Tommy Hayes was shot in the hip. Also on the way across they picked up thirty-eight bewildered Chinese prisoners, whom we could well have done without. No doubt this was the unfortunate group that Harold Mulry's 3 Platoon had chased off 1 Platoon's position and on to the road.

Shortly after this, US tanks rumbled into the re-entrant between C and A companies, whereupon Bob Murdoch with Nobby Clark and his bearers set to work loading wounded on to them. I was informed that the CO and the Intelligence Officer were with the tanks and that I was required there. My initial thought was that the CO had brought a small Tac HQ forward to take over command up front, but this was not so. At this conference he informed me that the Army Commander wanted to push 5 Regiment of the Cavalry Division forward to occupy the features on my left[17] but this was totally dependent on 3 RAR rifle companies holding the road from their overnight positions. He told me the Brigadier wanted B Company to return to the overnight position they had just vacated, and they were now in the process of doing that. He put it to me directly: "Would I stay another night?"

This put me in a rather invidious position. It was obviously an extremely important decision, one on which rested the next move of the Brigade and a Cavalry Regiment, and he was waiting for an answer. Many things went through my mind. The battered A Company would have to go into reserve and the untouched C Company brought forward. The forward positions would have to be thickened up with support from the Pioneer and Anti-Tank company platoons. There was a mass of artillery available now, which could be employed to tremendous advantage. Also, if the Cavalry Regiment was able to blast its way on to Sudok San, the enemy would have plenty to occupy his mind.

I told him we would stay, but on the strict proviso that B Company was back on the ground it had just given up, and the Cavalry Regiment was in occupation of the high ground west of us. If these provisions could not be met, an attempt had to be made to extract the rifle companies. At that time I did not appreciate that the party Gravener and the Chinese were having on 504 could escalate as it did, or my reply would have been emphatically in the negative.

The CO said he would get back to me, and departed with his tank to observe the outcome of the B Company attempt at returning to their ridge.

Battalion administration fell down completely. In addition to casualty evacuation I had requested resupply of essential items. All we received was a couple of boxes of Mk VIII Z belted MMG ammunition, dropped off by the tanks under the guns of the Chinese across the road. At considerable risk from enemy fire from across the road, George Harris, with Lofty Maletz and Vic Carr of 3 Platoon, recovered the ammunition. Vic Carr described the event:

> Once we had the ammo, four belts each, I ran the first 20 yards. Behind was Lofty, then came George. We had run a long way, about 400 yards, to reach cover of the spur and were under fire from the old B Company position. On climbing back up A Company feature, we had to pass through burning low scrub. Because of smoke plus the long run and weight of ammunition and weapon I began to falter and a number of men left their positions to come and help me.

Mk VIII Z was unsuitable for rifles and Bren guns due to the possibility of jamming in the breach.[18] Nevertheless, Harris had the belts stripped and the rounds distributed along with ammunition recovered from the casualties.

I had thought that the lack of resupply was due to tanks being the only means of getting through, and running stores is not proper employment for armour. However I was shocked recently to learn that, under instructions from WOII Darky Griffiths, a GMC driven by Claude Boshammer drove through to deliver ammunition to B Company prior to the arrival of the tanks.[19] This demonstrated that soft-skin vehicles could get through without drawing fire and I can now see no excuse at all for Battalion HQ not conducting normal resupply.

On his way to my location the CO had ordered B Company to reoccupy their overnight position. This instigated two costly attacks.

At the south end of the original B Company feature there was a low ridge which had been occupied by both sides at various times during the war, and in consequence was riddled with weapon pits, prompting the soldiers to dub it the "Honeycomb". 5 Platoon, commanded by Lt Ken McGregor, had just completed crossing the road in single file when Darcy Laughlin ordered them to return. Ken McGregor and his Platoon Sergeant, Uki Fraser, led a section across to secure the Honeycomb as the intermediate objective. Approaching the feature in extended line it soon became obvious the enemy had quickly followed B Company's departure, and occupied their ground. McGregor's platoon met a blast of machine-gun and rifle fire which quickly produced eight casualties, dead and wounded, including Lt Ken McGregor. Covering machine-gun fire was provided to extract this small group.

It was now clear that the Chinese were going to contest any attempt to regain control of the road. Darcy ordered Len Montgomery's 4 Platoon to take the Honeycomb. They fixed bayonets, ignored the firing directed at them and took the objective with a gallant fighting charge, but again at a cost in wounded and killed. From there it became abundantly clear that the Chinese now occupied the main feature in strength, and nothing short of a major battle would dislodge them. The attempt was aborted. The CO departed for the Middlesex Regiment and did not appear in the forward area again.

There is probably some excuse for Ken McGregor going

in unsupported, because he had just come off the Honeycomb and probably imagined it to be only lightly held, if at all. However, by the time Monty's platoon was committed, the enemy's intention to hold ground was clear. From daylight the NZ Regiment of 25-pounders was on line, and firing in support of D Company. Also in the area was a battalion of US 105s, and other US Army artillery — enough high explosive to blast the top off the hill and all available on request through Darcy's NZ fire controller, Lt Don Scott. When asked in subsequent correspondence why he did not shoot in support of the attack, Scott says he was not requested to do so.[20] In addition, there were fifteen US tanks in the battalion area, some observing the attack. One platoon of these could have walked Monty's men on to the objective. But despite an abundance of support the attacks went in cold. Again this conflicts with the statements that B Company had artillery support during the night. If so, the guns would have been registered to fire on the feature, and with minor adjustment could have supported Montgomery's attack.

At this time the CO had not officially handed command of the rifle companies to me, but, following his departure from the Honeycomb affair, I maintained close contact with them, particularly Gravener with his D Company under attack.

Meanwhile, back at D Company, the action against 12 Platoon persisted, with an attack every thirty minutes, each of which was met with effective artillery concentrations and the platoon's small-arms and mortar fire. Corporal Bill Rowlinson and his section took the brunt of the attacks and gave a fine account of themselves. Eventually the enemy gave up attacking on the narrow front and 12 Platoon observed them relocating their forming-up place and direction of attack. While the enemy was in the process of executing this manoeuvre, they were treated to five rounds of gunfire, which scattered them in all directions.[21]

Gravener reported that a potentially dangerous situation was developing. He suspected that the enemy was working around his right flank. He warned that they were coming close to what would be our withdrawal route, should this be ordered.

During the morning we were intrigued to observe a spotter aircraft fly over Hill 504 in company with three circling US Marine Corsair fighter aircraft, used in a close support role in Korea. We liked Corsairs supporting us because they flew low and slow and bombed accurately. Interest turned to horror when the spotter dropped a yellow target indicator spigot on Dave Mannett's 10 Platoon. The leading Corsair swooped in and released a napalm bomb, killing two men and horribly burning others before the pilot realised his error and aborted the attack. It is difficult to comprehend how this mistake could have occurred, as D Company was displaying fluorescent Ground to Air identification panels. Neither Norman nor I had requested the air strike nor could we find anyone who would admit responsibility for laying it on. Although wounded himself, the D Company Medic, Pte Ron Dunque, did outstanding work with the burn casualties.

The napalm attack on 10 Platoon brought confirmation that the enemy was working D Company's right flank. Seeking to take advantage of the confusion caused by the napalm, the enemy attacked Lt McWilliam's 11 Platoon from that direction, but they got it wrong and suffered a severe mauling.

During the afternoon Gravener decided to tighten his perimeter to meet a night defence situation by bringing 12 Platoon back to the company headquarters area. The Chinese occupied the recently evacuated 12 Platoon position and were kept very uncomfortable with artillery and fire from platoon weapons.

Shortly after the napalm incident the CO came on air to inform me that the 5th Cavalry Regiment would not be coming through to relieve us and I had approval to withdraw the rifle companies, and to exercise full command of them.

Anticipating that I would inherit this responsibility, the withdrawal had been occupying my thoughts for some time. The only practicable withdrawal route was to follow the narrow, four-kilometre-long wooded ridge line which ran south from Hill 504 to a ford just below the Middlesex Regiment. Of course there was a good possibility that the enemy had established a blocking force on it, but there was really no alternative.

Regarding the time of withdrawal, I selected 1600 hours. In this decision I was influenced by two considerations. The enemy had had all day to study us and it was an absolute certainty that come nightfall they would resume the attack. This time they would know precisely where and how to hit us, and if we were still around when it happened, withdrawal would be out. Second, I wanted two hours of daylight fields of fire so the Diggers could keep the enemy cautious and well away from the rear guard, hopefully long enough to get a clean break come dusk, permitting us to disappear into the night.

There were threats which had to be provided for. Movement of A, B or C companies up the hill had to be made in full view of the enemy on the low feature across the road, and without doubt they would cross over to cut up our tail. Also, up on the high ground D Company was very actively engaged with the opposition, making their extraction delicate and attracting close enemy follow-up. Then there was the question of a blocking force on the withdrawal route. The enemy group which Gravener reported as going round his right flank could easily be sitting there, or a force may have come across from the Chinese who had tangled with Support Company the previous night.

With H Hour decided, my withdrawal plan called for:

- neutralisation of the enemy on B Company's overnight position

- clearing the escape route
- withdrawal of rifle companies to fall-back positions behind D Company
- extraction of D Company
- leap-frog movement of the companies down the ridge to a ford just below the Middlesex Regiment.

At this time I was not aware that B Company had a FOO. They had not used guns on the Honeycomb so I assumed they did not have one. From the Middlesex position the Battery Commander had a line of sight to the Honeycomb feature, so I requested Ferguson to arrange for him to neutralise the enemy across the road, by laying down a smoke-screen to obscure our movements, and an extra dose of high explosive to anchor the enemy in their pits. The artillery was requested to open up at 1600 hours and this request was granted.

I ordered Darcy Laughlin to clear the escape route by beating his way down the ridge line from D Company to the ford below the Middlesex, commencing at 1600 hours. If he encountered the enemy, he was to attack and remove them. If he couldn't dislodge them, he was to keep them busy until I could get to him with a second company.

For extraction of D Company I instructed that C and A companies would be sited behind each other in blocking positions behind D, preparatory to extracting D Company. When moved, D Company was to take up defence behind A Company and so on. There was always one company in blocking defence, a second setting up behind it, and the third in movement to the next fall-back position. This leap-frog action was to be repeated all the way back to the ford. (See Map 20.)

In laying on the withdrawal I had omitted to cover the situation of having a large group of prisoners of war to plan for. I had completely forgotten about them. The Sergeant Major of B Company was a very large redhead, Blue Bradley, also referred to as the Red Steer. It seems

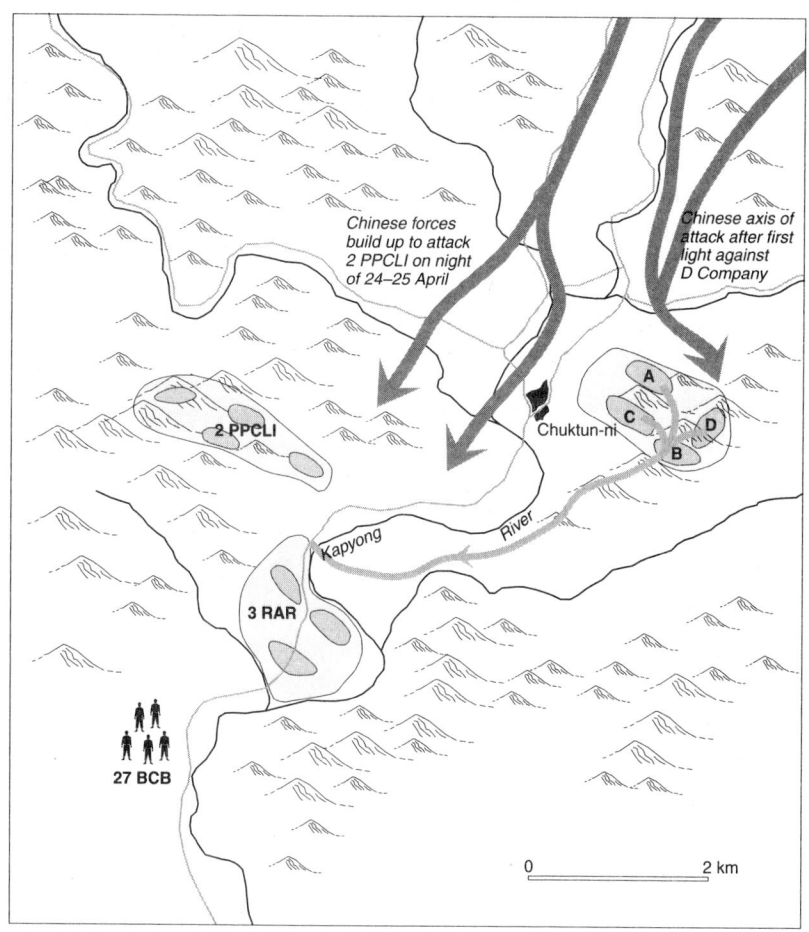

Map 20: 27 BCB situation, 24 April 1951

that this impressive man had become a father image to the prisoners. Don Parsons of C Company wrote:

> Another incident I recall was during the pull-out of 24 April. When we moved through B Company (or they moved through us) we were amused to see a large group of Chinese prisoners clustering around Blue Bradley, CSM B Coy. With his great height, red hair and pipe permanently in his mouth, he was probably the only Australian they could recognise and there was no way they were going to leave him.

On receiving his orders Darcy came back with, "What do I do with my prisoners?" Obviously the last thing needed in the midst of a column in an opposed withdrawal is thirty-eight of the enemy, particularly come nightfall. The alternatives were to turn them loose, shoot them or take them with us. They had been observing us all day and knew too much to turn them loose, and shooting them, apart from the humanitarian aspects, would not go over too well with the authorities. So I got back to Darcy and reminded him that he had captured them so he could look after them. He crossed me off his Christmas card list with a curt "Thanks a lot".

To give me mobility and control over the four rifle companies I handed command of A Company to Bob Murdoch, and created a small Tac HQ. I employed our 3 inch mortar fire controller, Ron Perkins, as my radio operator on the command net. Ron was a recent enlistment in the Australian Army but nevertheless a very experienced soldier. His previous service had been with the UK Army, in the Royal Marines and the Parachute Regiment.[22]

By 1600 hours all were in position and standing by. Even the enemy was cooperating, with a lull in proceedings. I sent B Company on their way in anticipation of artillery opening up as arranged. The minutes ticked by with no barrage banging away, and in this unhealthy silence I got an uneasy premonition that things were starting to go wrong. I tolerated the situation as long as I could before calling Colonel Ferguson for an explanation of this dreadful hiatus. He said he would check it out for me. Eventually he came back with the very unsatisfactory explanation that a wind change had necessitated the point of emission for smoke to be re-registered. I did not buy this, as they had had plenty of time to check registration. I believed there had been a stuff-up somewhere, and I was being shoved off with a weak excuse.

Much valuable daylight time was slipping by, so I

decided not to wait. I had already declared my hand by dispatching B Company so had nothing to loose by ordering Saunders to get C Company on its way to take up position behind D Company. By the time the tail of C Company was clear, tanks trundled into position on the road and manoeuvred to cover the enemy opposite us. I had not been informed that they would come to our assistance but could not have been more grateful for such timely intervention. I told Murdoch to get A Company moving and hurried off with Perkins to overtake and position C Company. Then the Kiwis let fly with smoke and high explosive, with a great heart-warming, thunderous thump, causing a tank to back off fast. I then knew the first phase would be accomplished without a hitch.

On reaching the top of the hill C and A companies were positioned to discourage follow-up by the enemy when D Company pulled back. I then ordered Gravener to withdraw. He replied that he could not do so because he was under attack again, so we just had to wait impatiently while he tidied up. Eventually he got an opportunity to thin out and the company took its departure. I led it back and located it it behind A Company, then withdrew C Company and sited it behind D Company, and in this way we rolled back, always one company in a blocking position and one in movement.

When the NZ Regiment Battery Commander, Maj Buzz Hunt, was advised we were clear of the D Company feature, he laid on a tremendous barrage, blanketing the whole area recently vacated. This sounded like a regimental concentration and had the effect of impeding enemy follow-up, ensuring the withdrawal got off to a good start. However, we could not deter the Chinese from leaning on us all the way down to the river.

About nightfall, a very welcome message arrived, reporting that B Company had reached the ford without locating enemy on the withdrawal route. This was a tremendous relief.

During the withdrawal process a surprising incident

occurred. Reconnaissance for fall-back positions and settling companies in necessitated me moving back and forth in the column. At one stage, after dark, I was horrified to find myself in the midst of a group of armed Chinese soldiers but very relieved to identify them as prisoners assisting the stretcher-bearers. I stopped the first escort to come my way and rather brusquely demanded to know why prisoners were bearing arms. The soldier responded immediately with the curt reply, "Well, you don't expect the bloody wounded to carry them, do you?" While I was digesting this piece of logic, the group disappeared into the gloom.

Eventually Ron Perkins and I arrived at the ford and met up with Lt Jim Young, acting 2 IC of B Company, who was checking the companies over. I recall having the grandfather of all headaches at this stage. B, C and D companies were clear, leaving Murdoch with A Company still in the last fall-back position. I called him up to check on the state of the game and got the unwelcome news that the opposition were still in attendance. I told him to make for the ford and shake them off if possible. The ford was a broad expanse of ankle-deep water, dangerously lit by a full moon, and an opposed crossing would produce many casualties. In due course Murdoch reported he was clear of his position and Jim and I waited, staring into the gloom in the expected direction of their approach.

Eventually Lou Brumfield's 2 Platoon arrived and we passed them over. Questioning the tail ender regarding the remainder of A Company I was informed that they were following him.

While Jim and I waited, bursts of machine-gun fire from the Princess Pats seemed to be perilously close, giving the impression that they were firing at A Company. I called the CO to get it stopped but was assured that the Canadians definitely had Chinese in their sights. Then the balance of A Company appeared, but from the wrong direction by ninety degrees, along the river edge. Bob told me he had lost the enemy so we passed the company over as rapidly as possible.

Bob Murdoch explained how he had shaken off the enemy. He made a mistake at a fork in the track and took the wrong turn, arriving at the river well short of the ford. Realising his error immediately, he swung the company hard left and continued on until he had located us. The Chinese, in hot pursuit, reached the river and finding no sign of A Company assumed they had crossed at that point and plunged in after them. This is what had prompted the Canadians to open up with their machine-guns. Bob wished he could claim his manoeuvre as a brilliant deception.

At the entrance to the Middlesex, the CO and some others from the Headquarters were checking troops into the area. I reported to the CO, I think about 2300 hours, that the withdrawal was complete and we had suffered no further casualties. This was not strictly true, for we discovered later that Pte Gwyther of D Company had been left behind. He lay stunned in a weapon pit and became a prisoner of war.

Events since the afternoon of the 23rd had once again demonstrated the great fighting spirit of the Australian Digger. In A Company they had taken on a very determined and numerically superior enemy, wave after wave. They had taken him on in the dark without artillery, mines, wire or any deterrent to the enemy attacks other than their personal weapons and guts. After each enemy attack they had removed the dead and wounded and occupied their pits to calmly await the next enemy onslaught and possibly a fate similar to the previous occupant. There was no hesitation on being placed in forward weapon pits; no man backed away as the enemy charged in. The next morning they were willing to go on with it and with bullet and bayonet drive the enemy from our ridge. Splendid men! The B Company men displayed the same unflinching gallantry when committed to two hopeless bayonet charges. In D

Company the Diggers had to tolerate the nerve-racking experience of a full day of continuous attack, made even more unpleasant by a napalm strike in their midst. All the companies then conduced a well-disciplined, close-quarters contact extraction.

Withdrawal is always a test of morale. It is instinctive for animal or man to put distance between himself and danger with as much speed as possible. With animal it is survival, but with soldiers it is fatal. In the withdrawal process, encumbered by the wounded, to run, or even to hurry, is disastrous and just what the enemy aims to achieve. The withdrawal at Kapyong was conducted by men who had been under extreme stress for a protracted period and a drop in morale might have been excused. But no excuse was necessary. The soldiers moved at a steady pace between fall-back positions, they took up blocking defence without discussion and waited for the enemy to appear. There was no suggestion of haste or a break in discipline. The withdrawal went off like a training exercise.

The men of Kapyong were magnificent. The Battle of Kapyong on 23–24 April was won by the fighting spirit of the Diggers.[23]

On the night of 24–25 April the Princes Pats held the line with a stubborn defensive action, even to the extent of bringing the artillery down on their forward weapon pits to hold the Chinese out.

These blocking actions stopped the enemy's momentum and bought time, at great cost in Australian and Canadian lives. This time gave the United Nations Command the opportunity to reorganise, and to position a force in the path of the Chinese Army, and Seoul was saved. In recognition of their gallantry, these battalions were awarded the United States Presidential Distinguished Unit Citation.

EPILOGUE

For some years after the Korean War I lost track of many of my old A Company comrades, due to a series of postings which kept me out of Australia or in areas where only limited contact could be maintained. However, eventually I caught up with Mick Servos, an old 2 Platoon man who went on to make WOII rank. On his retirement he became an inspector for the Income Tax Department in Brisbane. During a conversation in November 1988 it became evident that Mick had kept tabs on several old A Company villains, so I put it on him to assemble as many as possible for a drink and a yarn. The next day Mick rang to say a meeting was arranged for the following night at the Battle of Waterloo Hotel. Somehow, even with such short notice, he had been able to gather fifteen to twenty old hands.

We had a pleasant night becoming reacquainted and remembering friends and incidents from our Korea days. I suggested to Mick that we should meet on a regular basis. Mick Servos did not stop there, for he was a very efficient and tireless organiser. From that meeting he went on to form the national 3 RAR Association and to produce a journal titled *Old Faithful*, the title bestowed on 3 RAR by Lt Gen Sir Thomas Daly KBE CB DSO. Through the years Mick's Association has performed the invaluable service of keeping 3 RAR veterans in touch with each other. It now has hundreds of members from all parts of Australia.

For the fiftieth anniversary of the Royal Australian Regiment a committee was established, under the presidency of Alf Handley, to create a National Memorial Walk, dedicated to members of the Regiment who died during overseas service. Following much organising and fundraising this dream came to fruition at the Enoggera Army Barracks, Brisbane, in November 1998. The walk consists of a "meditation" building and one thousand trees; a plaque bearing a deceased soldier's name will be placed at the foot of each tree. Mick, as project manager, threw himself into this enterprise, but the organising and negotiating had a detrimental effect on his health, to the extent that he was hospitalised for most of the opening ceremonies. Health has now forced his retirement. We veterans owe much to Mick Servos; his will be a hard act to follow.

Mick was fortunate that he had some good back-stops with him, particularly Ron Perkins. Without making a great fuss about it, Ron has put a tremendous amount of effort into ensuring the success of the 3 RAR Association. Fortunately he is still in very good shape. Ron is the soldier who operated my command net radio during the withdrawal at Kapyong. He went on to make a career in the army and served with the AATTV in Vietnam. He was granted a Regular Army commission and retired at the rank of Major. Following his army service he became secretary of the Townsville Fire Brigade, before heading up his own business servicing heavy vehicles. At the 1999 annual general meeting of the 3 RAR Association Ron was unanimously voted in as President.

Vic Carr is an old 2 Platoon comrade of Mick Servos. Vic was a member of 2 Platoon when it left Japan in September 1950. By the time he had completed his Korean service he had been in every 3 RAR action and was the only original 1950 veteran remaining in 2 Platoon. On his return to Australia Mick and Vic did a posting together at the Airborne Platoon, RAAF

Williamstown. After leaving the army Vic became involved with the timber industry. Wherever old 3 RAR veterans are assembled, there you will find his cheerful face.

My first 2iC, Algy Clark, was with me for only a few weeks before his recall to Australia. Eventually he commanded the SAS Regiment and retired as a Colonel and settled in the West. I had had reports that he was in poor physical condition, but I was pleasantly surprised to see him at a reunion in Brisbane, in November 1998, glass in hand. As with Mark Twain, reports of his condition were exaggerated.

My second 2iC, Reg Saunders, left the service for a position with the Department of Aboriginal Affairs, in Canberra, and on the Council of the Australian War Memorial. On most visits to the ACT I would contact him and we would discuss this and that over a glass of ale. A few years back I received a message advising that he had been admitted to the Canberra Hospital and would not be walking out of it. I made an immediate trip to Canberra to check him out, and another a fortnight later for his funeral. The church was packed for the service and overflowed to a large crowd outside. Those attending represented all ranks of the regiment, including a number of generals. At the crematorium I discovered that the didgeridoo could be a sensitive, lyrical instrument, capable of soulful, moving music.

Captain Bob Murdoch was my 2iC at Kapyong. We renewed our friendship a few years later, when on a course at the School of Tactics and Administration, but our paths did not cross again. Some years later I got a line on him in Western Australia and tried to make contact. However, I was saddened to learn that he was afflicted with motor neurone disease and unable to speak on the telephone.

John Church, who commanded 2 Platoon and was wounded at Chisan, continued with his military career and retired a Colonel with a DSO. In 1954 he did me the honour of being Best Man at my wedding. He is settled in Canberra and we meet occasionally.

Harold Mulry, to whom I owed so much, served on for some time before leaving the army. Though we had telephone contact from time to time I physically caught up with him and his wife only once, when they visited Melbourne for the Cup. Since then his wife has died and Harold is settled in Tasmania, in Launceston where he has a daughter.

I had a brief encounter with Fred Gardiner, when we accidentally ran into each other in a Sydney street many years ago. He looked well enough at the time but shortly after I received an unconfirmed report of his death.

Lou Brumfield went on to successfully command the first Australian battalion to be committed to the Vietnam War, 1 RAR. He retired as a Brigadier with a CBE and DSO and resides on the Gold Coast. He keeps himself fit and we meet on a fairly regular basis, at reunions, parades and the like.

On my return to Australia I did a short stint with 4 RAR, waiting clearance for posting to Malaya. Angus McDonald was also with 4 RAR at that time, and we had the usual association in the officers mess. This was my last contact with him as he died shortly after my return to Australia in 1954.

Tom Muggleton, our Company Sergeant Major, went on to become the Regimental Sergeant Major at the Royal Military College, Duntroon. He later received a Quartermaster Commission and went to Vietnam with 5 RAR, as their Quartermaster. Following military service he went on the staff of the Bills and Papers Office at Parliament House, Canberra. He is now retired on the Gold Coast.

Of the five who were taken prisoner at Ichon, Angus McDonald and Tom Hollis are the only ones I have run across. I meet Tom Hollis at the 3 RAR Kapyong Day Parade. I have tried to talk him into putting down his experiences as a prisoner of the North Korean Army but without success. It is a pity, as there is a story there which needs to be told.

Vic Svenson continued in the Regular Army and we served together again when we recreated Battle Wing of the Jungle Training Centre, Canungra, in November 1954. Later Vic served in Vietnam with the AATTV before being granted a Quartermaster Commission. He retired in Townsville, and we meet fairly often at reunions and parades. He is as fit as he ever was. Well, almost.

George Harris served on in the Regular Army and saw service in Vietnam with the AATTV in 1964–65 and again in 1966–67 where he was Mentioned in Dispatches, and awarded the Cross of Gallantry twice and the Honour Medal twice. On leaving the army he was a security officer for Safeways and Woolworths supermarket outlets for sixteen years. He lived in an adjoining suburb to me, and our contact was reasonably frequent. Along with Tommy Hayes and some others we used to visit the Recruit Training Battalion at Kapooka, to lend moral support to the Kapyong Platoon. George died at the end of 1999.

Allan (Hoagie) Carmichael made it to Sergeant and was one of those selected to represent Australia at the Peace Celebrations in America and the United Kingdom, following the end of the Korean War.

There was a follow-up to the attack on Woodbine, Hill 410, when I was able to assist three of the casualties of this action with representation to the Department of Veterans' Affairs. Fit young men recover rapidly from their injuries and keenly get on with living, either by "soldiering on" or returning to civilian life. However, in their late fifties and sixties the veterans' old injuries can tend to flare up, depleting the quality of life, and some veterans have difficulty in getting their problems recognised by the Department of Veterans' Affairs. The problem is greatest for the uncomplaining soldiers who have not established a medical history by whinging to the RMO at every ache or pain. Such was the case with three of the casualties of the 410 attack: 3 Platoon Sergeant, Charlie Scholl, Radio Operator, Brian (Lofty) Hewiston, and RAAMC Medic, Sydney (Nobby) Clark.

Some years ago it was drawn to my attention that Charlie Scholl's back wound was giving him trouble, but he was getting no assistance from Veterans' Affairs for the medical expenses involved. Consistent with his uncomplaining nature he had accepted this state of affairs. I advised him to get a specialist report on the injury and appeal the ruling. This he did but the report, although technically sound, did not relate the problem to the wounding, and Charlie got nowhere. At a function at 3 RAR I brought the matter up with Gen Jim Connolly, AO, and he asked me to write up the circumstances of the case for him. From there this busy general found the time to take action on Charlie's behalf, and brought the subject to a happy conclusion.

Charlie "soldiered on" until 1973, when he headed back to the land, and for a time worked on a quarry crusher. When he gave that up he put all his effort into producing fruit and vegetables on his double block in Urinquinty, New South Wales. He is now troubled by his back and leg and has decided to give the hard work away and relax a little. Somehow I can't get a mental picture of Charlie Scholl sitting out his time snoring on the cool side of the house.

Similarly, by 1995 the back injury sustained by Brian Hewiston when he took a fall on the "Slippery Slide" was causing him considerable discomfort. Again his approach to Veterans' Affairs fell on deaf ears. The problem was that when a company takes a beating as we did on 410, resulting in many battle casualties, those with non-battle injuries tend to play down their problems and grin and bear it. Thus Lofty did not establish a medical history at the time, and did not haunt the RAP subsequently. Fortunately Ossie Osbaldiston and I were able to provide supporting statements which helped to resolve the matter.

Our RAAMC Medic, Nobby Clark, also had a problem. He too took a fall down the slippery surface where we all had a problem with footing. At that time he hurt his back and hip. During the attack next morning Allan Cardinal was wounded and went rolling down hill. To save him from further damage Nobby grabbed him, and the impact and momentum rocketed the pair downhill before Nobby could gain control. Later Nobby told me he had hurt himself but had to remain on duty because he was our only RAAMC Medic. I was able to support his application with a statement confirming the situation.

Nobby "soldiered on" for thirty-nine years, including three and a half years of World War II, twenty-nine and a half Regular Army and six in the Reserve.

I caught up with Roy Nunan a couple of years after Korea in Sydney. I was aware that he was working at the Newtown RSL as a barman and it so happened that John Callander and I, in full uniform, were proceeding through Sydney by taxi and came across this RSL. We pulled over and entered and there was my ex-orderly behind the bar, attending to a group of thirsty veterans. I attracted his attention by calling out sharply, "Nunan!" In surprise he dropped a glass and responded instinctively, "Sir!" This drew immediate reaction from the drinkers. "Sir. Sir! Is that how you crawled your way through Korea?" It was probably the only time he ever called me "Sir" — usually it was Skipper or Boss. Roy threw off his apron and we took him into the city with us.

Roy's gone now where no one is going to criticise the state of his Owen gun.

Sgt Jim Everleigh, who performed so gallantly for the company, was eventually awarded a Military Medal. Our paths did not cross after Korea, and the first line I got on him was the notice of his death in Canberra.

I caught up with my second driver, Robert (Abdul) Guest, some years ago when he was still in pretty good shape. However, a severe stroke means that he now gets around in a motorised wheelchair. I last saw him at George Harris's funeral and he was as cheerful as ever!

In the account of the action at Kapyong I reported that Tom Hayes was wounded during the B company withdrawal across the road. There was an interesting follow-up to that incident. Attached to the battalion was a Visitors and Observers Section which looked after war correspondents, visiting VIPs and such. Tom came forward at Kapyong with Ian Reid, the representative for the Melbourne *Herald* and the Sydney *Sun*. Through some mix-up Tom got stranded in B Company and was allocated to a rifle section to make up the numbers. He remained with them and was wounded, shot in the thigh.

When the US Presidential Citation was awarded to the battalion, every member who participated in the battle was awarded the Citation for life. The Routine Order setting out the ground rules for qualification limited entitlement to those on the posted strength of 3 RAR, on 23–24 April 1951. Tom was not on the battalion nominal roll and was refused the Citation on those grounds. In spite of repeated representations by me and others we could not get Army Headquarters to relent, even though he had served with the battalion as a rifleman at Kapyong, and been wounded in the process. When I was on Army Headquarters there was an axiom: "It doesn't have to make sense. It's policy."

My company radio operator, Ossie Osbaldiston, is still in good shape and as fierce as ever. After Korean service he took a discharge and went back to continue his career in the wool trade.

I catch up with Ted (Lofty) Maletz on an annual basis, at a function laid on by the Korean community of Southport, Queensland. The years have been kind to him, and he is much the same as ever.

Pat Knowles, a member of 1 Platoon, is always at the 3 RAR Kapyong Parade at Holsworthy. He is notorious as the member of A Company who has put pen to paper more than any other. He writes a good yarn, if somewhat highly imaginative.

Of my cooks, Cliff Muncy continued with a career in the Army Catering Corps, eventually making the rank of Major. Our paths crossed on several occasions. Claude Boshammer was Lt Col Green's driver then went on to Headquarters Company. He was the driver who brought a GMC through at Kapyong. Nick Thorley setled in Melbourne and, through regular contact, keeps me up to date with certain of the old crew. I fear he has a large telephone bill.

Being heavily reinforced after the Pakchon battle, the officers and soldiers were pretty much strangers to each other. However, the harsh living conditions of the following months, and soldiering on mobile operations in sub-zero conditions, forced a dependence on one another. Add to this the actions of Tokchong, Doctor, Hill 410, Chisan, Sardine and Kapyong and we bonded into a tightly knit team. When we of that period met, we do so as family.

APPENDIX A:
OVERTURE TO BATTLE:
The audacity of Ridgway

by Jack Gallaway

During the second week of April 1951, Eight Army completed Operation Rugged, an advance designed to place the United Nations forces on Line Kansas, a line which roughly coincided with the 38th Parallel, where it was planned they should hold. (See Map 14.) In an endeavour to cause maximum damage to the communist forces, a further advance was undertaken towards what was known as the Iron Triangle, a supply base and assembly region for Chinese reinforcements, the objectives of this further advance being Line Wyoming.

During these advances, many Chinese and North Korean prisoners were taken, and through the identification of units and other means, American intelligence developed a fairly accurate picture of the Chinese deployment. It was a fairly ominous line-up — roughly twenty-seven divisions or 270,000 men. The prisoners boasted of a coming Spring offensive, and many of them were willing to provide their interrogators with a remarkably accurate prediction of the date — 22 April.[1]

Gen Ridgway accepted this information as being accurate, and his planners prepared Plan Audacious as a counter measure.[2] Under Audacious, 1 Corps had the responsibility for holding the South Korean capitol, Seoul, and with its left bank anchored on the Imjim River, it was provided with sufficient strength to make that portion of the defensive line virtually impregnable — three divisions of US troops plus one ROK Division, the Turkish Brigade Group and the powerful British 29th Brigade Group. I Corp's right flank would be held by 24 US Division. IX Corps would be their neighbour, and on their left flank 6 ROK Division would be responsible for almost sixteen kilometres of front, being flanked on its right by the tough, battle-hardened 1 US Marines. The length of front for which these two divisions were responsible was greater than that held by I Corps.[3] The area covered by 6 ROK also included the route taken by the force which outflanked Seoul three months earlier, when the city fell to the Chinese on 4 January.[4]

1 Cavalry Division, under command of I Corps, was withdrawn from the line and deployed in the north-east of Uijongbu, dispersed and camouflaged.[5] The only reserve available to IX Corps was the 27th British Commonwealth Brigade. Two battalions then with the brigade, 3 RAR and 2 PPCLI, had been responsible for taking the features which formed that portion of Line Kansas on their front. After months of heavy fighting they had been withdrawn for rest and reorganisation and were deployed in a salubrious area near the town of Kapyong.[6]

Plan Audacious called for the Chinese to make a maximum effort at the weakest point in the line and it was obvious this was the section held by 6 ROK. It was required that the line would withdraw under this pressure and 24 Division and 1 US Marines would refuse their flanks, thus sucking vast numbers of Chinese into a deep salient. At the appropriate juncture, and in the best American tradition, the cavalry would arrive. 1 Cavalry Division, heavily reinforced with tanks and artillery,[7] would drive east to join up with 1 Marine Division and these two formations would crush the Chinese between them. (See Map 15.)

During the second week in April, General MacArthur was sacked, and Ridgway was appointed to command the

UN Forces. Just prior to his departure for Tokyo, Ridgway held a conference at Yoju on 13 April. It was attended by senior Eighth Army staff and his three Corps Commanders, Lieutenant Generals Milburn, Hoge and Almond. Ridgway appraised his senior generals of the impending arrival of Van Fleet to take command of the Eighth Army, warning them that a massive CCF attack could occur at any hour and that they should be prepared to put Plan Audacious into effect on army command.[8] If it all worked for him, Ridgway would sustain a major victory and possibly kill sufficient enemy as to break the will of the CCF. If anything went awry, however, there existed a strong possibility that thousands of angry Chinese would pour down the Kapyong Valley and threaten the road and rail system that sustained the Eighth Army. Should this occur, the only troops who would stand in front of these hordes would be the men of 27th British Commonwealth Brigade, and due to breakdown in communications, they were in total ignorance of the General's plans.[9]

On 13 April, while Ridgway was briefing his generals, 27 BCB was under command of 24 Division, I Corps, and engaged in securing "Sardine" and "Salmon", and placing the brigade on the Kansas Line. Two days later the brigade handed the positions over to 6 ROK Division and moved into reserve at Kapyong. 27 BCB was about to disappear from the United Nations line of battle. Brigade Headquarters and two British battalions, 1 Middlesex and 1 Argyle and Sutherland Highlanders, would return to Hong Kong and part of their replacements, 28 BCB HQ, the 1 King's Own Scottish Borderers, were already in the country.[10]

Ridgway briefed only his corps commanders at the conference on 13 April. It must be assumed that they then went to brief their Divisional commanders at some time consequent to that.

In modern parlance, 27 British Commonwealth Brigade was "out of the loop" in the briefing process. At the same time, the need to attend to administrative matters associated with the changeover would have absorbed the Brigade Commander's attention and that of his staff to the exclusion of operational matters. Briefed on 13 April, it is likely the corps commanders briefed their divisional commanders on the 14th or the 15th. Since he was under command of 24 Division, Col Bourke, acting commander of 27 BCB, would not have been invited to this gathering. When the GOC 24 Division held a similar briefing for his regimental commanders, however, 27 BCB was no longer under command.

Once in Corps reserve, the only source from which the Brigade Commander or his staff could have obtained this information would have been IX Corps. Since they were deployed for administrative reasons rather than operational purposes, it seems certain that they escaped the notice of those at Corps who could have enlightened them, and since they knew nothing of any pending enemy offensive, they would not have had any reason to ask.

It seems certain that the change in the circumstances of 27 BCB from under Divisional Command in I Corps to Corps Reserve on IX Corps removed Bourke from the chain of communications and left him and his battalion commanders in total ignorance of the true situation at the most critical point of the battle.

APPENDIX B:
RIFLE COMPANY BATTLE CASUALTIES, SEPTEMBER 1950 TO APRIL 1951

Casualties for rifle companies and attached personnel

Company	Killed in action	Wounded in action	POW	Total
A	51	114	5	170
B	13	39		52
C	3	21		24
D	18	64	1	83

Killed in action, A Company and attached personnel (In order of occurrence)

6/47	Lt	J.F. Wathen	3/400190	Pte	W.E. Jillett
1/00001	Cpl	M.B. Hogden	1/400045	Pte	P.A. Farquarson
2/400095	Pte	L.V. Maher	5/400096	Pte	J.A. Atkinson
2/874	WOII	D. McGavin	3/400220	Pte	L.A. Jones
1/400015	Pte	R.L. Hannify	2/400011	Pte	B.J. Goldsmith
2/3247	Pte	J.H. Simpson	1/9915	Sgt	S.K. Lenoy
1/00009	L/Cpl	F.J. Origlasso	3/1927	Pte	G.C. Pretty
2/140	Pte	E.W. Buckless	1/1130	Pte	K.G. O'Connor
2/400103	L/Cpl	J.K. Andrew	2/400088	Pte	A. Harris
5/400017	Pte	J. Richardson	2/2563	Cpl	L.A. Lowe
1/400038	Pte	D. McEwen	1/400121	Pte	L.B. Smeaton
3/400225	Pte	D. Bromley	1/1028	L/Cpl	D. Koosney
1/400132	Pte	H.L. Leaney	2/400018	Pte	G.H. Paterson
1/341	Sgt	V.T. Healy	2/400028	Pte	P. Clist
1/400143	Pte	M.A. Woods	1/400059	Pte	T.O. Barton
1/400064	Pte	T.S. Smith	1/1189	Sgt	J.T. Sheppard (MM)
1/9690	Pte	A. Mealing	3/400163	Pte	L.B. Theisinger
1/400104	Pte	W.D. Hoare	2/400048	Pte	T.W. Walter

APPENDIX B *201*

2/2263	Cpl	J.McK. Tannock	2/400361	Pte	D.G. Stewart
5/1274	Pte	P.L. Judd	4/400057	Pte	D. Bridge
1/400156	Pte	R. Fisher	3/400203	Pte	H. Bolitho
2/3090	L/Cpl	N.C. Worth	4/943	Pte	G.H. Harris
2/3243	Pte	T.J. Flanagan	3/400258	Pte	C.B. Looker
2/400023	Pte	J.W. Carter	NZ Arty	Lt	D. Fielding
2/400245	Pte	R.A. Ingram	NZ Arty	Gnr	Kemp
2/400129	Pte	A.G. Rimmer			

Wounded in action A Company and attached personnel (in order of occurrence)

Note: Some men were wounded more than once.

2/400128	Pte	D.L. Kerr	2/5486	Pte	J.W. Rogers
2/400047	Pte	K.J. Williams	1/400013	Pte	J.I. Condon
2/400067	Pte	P.O. Trump	1/400245	Pte	G.A.C. Houston
2/400120	Pte	Y.A. Norton	3/400245	Pte	L. Mooney
2/1161	Cpl	R.R. Burns	4/650	Pte	E.P. Fuller
1/400026	Pte	R.J. Peskett	2/400170	Pte	C.G. Finch
1/400018	Pte	L.G. Gagen	4/400005	Pte	E.J. Brown
2/400026	Pte	T.D. Docherty	6/400000	Cpl	L.E. Ray
2/400024	Cpl	L.E. Buckland	2/400361	Pte	D.G. Stewart
2/400147	Pte	E.A. Wallace	2/400202	Pte	D. Bennett
1/400001	Cpl	M.B. Hogden	5/400073	L/Cpl	V.J. Cleghorn
3/40021	Capt	W.J. Chitts	2/400376	Pte	T.F. Coffey
2/45157	Sgt	H.E. Brivis	3/400087	Pte	J.W. Gason
1/400028	Pte	L. Lyons	3/400208	Pte	R.G. Maynard
1/400050	Pte	D.D. Jenkins	4/400062	L/Cpl	W.W. Sinclair
1/400029	Pte	J.W. Goldsmith	1/400067	Pte	N.J. Derrington
2/400257	Pte	T.O. Watson	3/400221	Pte	M.C. Douglas
2/400036	Pte	W.J. Jones	5/400033	Pte	J.H. MacKay
1/400022	Pte	M. Servos	5/400065	Pte	W.N. Norman
3/400165	Pte	J.A. Annear	3/400123	Pte	B.G. Hewiston
2/400245	Pte	R. Ingram	1/400011	Pte	I. Richardson
5/400072	Pte	K.J. Brooks	2/400000	Cpl	D.P. Buck
2/400170	Pte	C.G. Finch	1/400024	Pte	L.J. Hutley
5/400016	Pte	H.R. Horwood	2/400242	Pte	A.R. Caldwell
3/400123	Pte	B.G. Heweston	2/3668	Cpl	G. MacKenzie
1/400069	Pte	E.R. Smith	4/400038	Pte	K.W. Magin
1/400140	Pte	J. Geedrick	1/400038	Pte	R.M. Crisp
1/400070	Pte	N.G. Costigan	2/400081	Pte	C.C. Anderson
2/400288	Pte	J.W. Connolly	2/400019	Cpl	E. Pearson
2/400134	Pte	J.F. Eshlin	1/400000	L/Cpl	W.R. McHenry
2/400140	Pte	M.H. Byrnes	1/339	Pte	C.D. Donovan
1/9152	Pte	J.E. Eade	2/35007	Lt	N.R. Charlesworth
2/3573	Cpl	S. Newell	1/400003	Pte	E. Maletz

1/400055	Pte	F. Williams	5/7005	Lt	J.M. Church
1/400023	Pte	A.K. Sutherland	5/5709	Maj	B.S. O'Dowd
2/400104	Pte	G.A. Butler	1/400071	Pte	L.G. Gallagher
2/400025	Pte	J.C. Forrest	5/400043	Pte	G.V.R. McGovern
1/1153	Pte	J.W. Zalewiski	2/400136	Pte	G.R. Yea
3/897	Sgt	G.D. Harris	2/400303	Pte	H.G. Brooks
1/400059	Pte	T.D. Barton	4/400045	Pte	A.C. Breuer
5/400014	Pte	R.C. Sheppard	6/400003	Pte	F.L.D. McGough
3/400021	Cpl	J.C.R. Carter	5/400021	Pte	J.T. Lawson
3/400199	Pte	R.A. Slade	2/400170	Pte	C.G. Finch
5/400036	Pte	T.W. Harris	2/400247	Pte	R.K. Cullen
1/400069	Pte	E.R. Smith	5/400057	Pte	T.F. Conlon
3/1927	L/Cpl	G.C. Pretty	3/1848	Pte	R.M. Grima
1/400061	Pte	J.J. Minehan	2/400200	Pte	R. Holloway
1/400048	Cpl	A. Carmichael	2/400121	Pte	S.R. Waldron
1/400065	Cpl	C. Scholl	1/400088	Pte	T. Allebone
2/400355	Pte	R. Hendricks	4/400038	Pte	K.W. Magin
2/400216	Pte	M. Hyham	1/400065	Pte	A. Prior
1/339	Cpl	C.D. Donovan	1/340	L/Cpl	G.R. MacKay
1/400123	Pte	C.B. Learmonth	1/1039	Pte	R.K. Duell

Prisoners of war, A Company and attached personnel

1/400127	Lt	A.P. McDonald	2/400024	Cpl	L.E. Buckland
2/400000	Cpl	D.P. Buck	2/400311	Pte	T.H.J. Hollis
1/400059	Pte	E.G. Light			

NOTES

1. To Korea

1. A tracked vehicle with steel body armour capable of stopping small-arms bullets only.
2. 3 RAR War Diary, 17 October 1950.
3. 3 RAR War Diary, 17 October 1950.
4. Ibid., 21 October 1950.
5. Ibid., 21–22 October 1950.
6. Ibid., 25 October 1950.
7. The previous commander, Maj (Speed) Gordon, had been injured when his jeep was swiped off the road by a US tank.
8. 3 RAR War Diary, 28–29 October 1950.

2. The Battle of Pakchon

1. Taped record, Walsh to Jack Gallaway, in 3 RAR Museum.
2. See article by Brig Wilson in Regimental journal, *Duty First*, Vol. 2, No. 5, Spring 1997.
3. See letter, L. G. Clarke to Jack Gallaway, in 3 RAR Museum.
4. Report by Capt Cyril Hall, in 3 RAR Museum.
5. Digger's nickname for an Asian.

3. Assembling the team

1. While checking telephone lines Slim was taken prisoner during the fighting at the Battle of Kapyong and died while a POW. He received a posthumous George Cross for the example he set as a prisoner.

4. The running-in phase

1. A nickname the Diggers ascribed to any Asian, not necessarily in a derogatory sense.
2. 3 RAR War Diary, 19 November 1950.

5. Running away

1. 3 RAR War Diary, 1 December 1950.

6. The Bridge at Yopa-ri

1. The War Diary says "Defensive Fire" but this is incorrect. Forward Observation Officers were not allocated and harassing fire was being organised from somewhere over the river, into the high ground above us.
2. We went into the operation stripped to "battle order" with no protection from the cold. If we'd stamped our feet in the snow for over twelve hours we would have been very cold indeed.

8. Activities at Uijongbu

1. KMAG: Korean Military Adviser Group. ROK commanders had their hands held by a US Army KMAG officer.
2. Each company clerk had a steel box containing roll books, sick reports, charge sheets and other types of stationery necessary for general administration.

9. Tokchong: a perilous withdrawal

1. This was a preview of how this division was to perform at Kapyong in the following April.

10. On the run again

1. 3 RAR War Diary, 3 January 1951.

11. Thirty-two kilometres of no man's land

1. Reg and I maintained a friendship up to the time of his death, when he was given a fittingly emotional service, attended by a huge crowd of mourners, from generals down.
2. 3 RAR Patrol Order No. 7, 14 January 1951. AWM 85 4/25.
3. 3 RAR War Diary, 16 January 1951.

12. Patrol to Ichon

1. 3 RAR Patrol Order No. 10, 19 January 1951. AWM 85 4/25. This written order makes no mention of patrolling across the valley. The CO gave me this task in a verbal instruction immediately prior to our departure.

2. L/Cpl John Andrew, ex Royal Marines World War II.
3. See article by John Church in *Duty First*, Vol. 2, No. 2, March 1996.
4. My orders to McDonald did not include taking prisoners, but one of the occupants of the hut could have supplied the information to satisfy the CO's requirement.

13. Patrol to Chipyong-ni

1. John Church, *Duty First*, Vol. 2, No. 2, March 1996.

14. Attack on Hill 195, "Doctor"

1. See article by John Church in *Duty First*, Vol. 2, No. 2, March 1996.
2. Cpl J.T. Sheppard won his MM in World War II during the Battle of Tobruk.
3. 3 RAR War Diary.

15. Attack on Hill 410, "Woodbine"

1. 3 RAR War Diary, 6–7 March 1951.
2. See article by George Harris in 3 RAR Journal, *Old Faithful*, April 1998, 155S.
3. Ibid.
4. 3 RAR War Diary, 7 March 1951.

16. The God Botherers

1. Chaplain W. T. Cummings, sermon on Battan, March 1942.

19. Attack on "Sardine"

1. See George Harris's account of this action in 3 RAR Association Journal, *Old Faithful*, Vol. 1, No. 36, April 1998.

21. The Battle of Kapyong

1. E8 Shermans were equipped with a 76 mm HV main armament and 2×30 and 1×50 cal mm.
2. Office, Chief of Army Field Forces, Fort Monroe, Virginia. Training Bulletin No. 2, February–March 1992.
3. 27 British Commonwealth Brigade War Diary. Copy in 3 RAR Museum.
4. C. Blair, *The Forgotten War*, Doubleday, NY, 1989.
5. Account by C. McGregor, "With the Australians in Korea", Norman Bartlett WM Publication, p. 92.

6. Lou Brumfield went on to command the first Australian Battalion to serve in Vietnam, where he was awarded the DSO. He retired a Brigadier with a CBE.
7. We had done this successfully in January during the evacuation of Seoul.
8. C. Luskie, 40 Oakley Street, Cummock, NSW 2867.
9. K. Hatfield, 15 Central Avenue, Seaholme, Vic 3018.
10. C. Kealy, 9 Waller Street, Shortland, NSW 2307.
11. After Action Report, 3 RAR Museum.
12. Capt Bennett, a graduate of the RMC, Chief of the Joint Services staff and later Governor of Tasmania, Sir Philip.
13. Lindsay Beek, 241 Fifth Street, Geraldton, WA 6530. Taped interview, in 3 RAR Museum.
14. Ibid.
15. Letter from 3 RAR Adjutant (Capt Len Eyles) to Jack Gallaway, in 3 RAR Museum.
16. Taped interviews with Hatfield and Osbaldiston, in 3 RAR Museum.
17. So much for the grandiose role allocated by Audacious. In fact a study of the distance to be covered and the nature of the terrain makes execution of the Cavalry Division's original task very doubtful.
18. Mk VIII .303 ammunition was developed for use in Medium Machine Guns. It uses a more powerful propellant than the standard rifle. If used in a rifle the expended cartridge case can jam in the breach.
19. C. Boshammer, 3 MacIntosh Street, Gympie, Qld 4570. Taped interview, in 3 RAR Museum. Telephone conversation with WOII Griffiths confirmed Boshammer's statement.
20. See correspondence between Scott and Jack Gallaway, in 3 RAR Museum.
21. Gravener's After Action Report, AWM.
22. Ron Perkins later was granted a Regular Commission and retired with the rank of Major.
23. Ian McGibbon, *New Zealand and the Korean War*, Vol. II, Oxford University Press, Auckland, p. 137. McGibbon took exception to my statement that the "Diggers won the battle of Kapyong". Clearly my intention was to imply that the battle was not won by clever officer decisions or cunning tactical moves, but by the sheer guts and determination of the Australian soldier. McGibbon reads "Digger" as "3 RAR" winning the Battle of Kapyong to the exclusion of credit to the Princes Pats and the NZ Field Regiment. Apparently the New Zealanders are touchy about being excluded from the US Presidential Distinguished Unit Citation.

Appendix A: Overture to battle

1. Clayton Blair, *The Forgotten War*, Doubleday, NY, 1989, p. 794 et seq. Notes 87 and 89 taken from memo in Ridgway's diary for 13 April. Ridgway's special file. (Blair was Ridgway's biographer.)
2. Ibid., pp. 794, 804, 819, 823–33, 840.
3. Ibid., pp. 1128–29. There were three Corps in Korea, the First, the Ninth and the Tenth, but the First Corps was always referred to by its Roman alphabetical index, and pronounced "Eye" Corps.
4. Ibid, p. 592 et seq. At Kapyong, 6 ROK was on the right flank of IX Corps adjoining I Corps whose right flank was held by 1 ROK Division which also bugged out.
5. Ibid., p. 804.
6. Ibid., p. 831.
7. Ibid., pp. 576–77. From early January, the US Forces had been heavily reinforced with Artillery. By April, each of seven divisions had four battalions of 105 Howitzers. In addition, two battalions of eight-inch howitzers, and seven equipped with guns or howitzers of 155 mm calibre, were available to Corps and Army levels.
8. *The Forgotten War*, pp. 831–32.
9. Ibid.
10. Ibid.

INDEX

187 Airborne RCT 10, 11
2/11 Aust Inf Bn 3
Itape–Wewak 3
Anderson, (Jock) Pte 49
Andrew, J. K. (Jim) Cpl 97
Apple Orchard Battle 11
Argent, A. (Alf) Lt 21, 143
Argyll & Sutherland Highlanders 2, 9, 10, 14, 18, 49, 52, 91, 150

Bagnall, A. J. (Jack) Cpl 135
Baker, B. (Brian) Pte 108
Beacroft, E. C. (Teddy) Lt 32
Beard, D. D. (Don) Capt 62, 89, 90, 108, 143
Beavis, H. E. (Knoogie) Sgt 29
Beeck, L. G. (Lindsay) Cpl 173
Bennett, P. H. (Phil) Capt 166
Bewley, A. A. (Bert) Pte 127
Bolitho, H. (Harry) Pte 154, 168
Boshammer R. C. (Claude) Pte 176
Bradley, E. (Bluey) WOII 180, 181
Broken Bridge Battle 14
Brown, W. F. (Wally) Maj 12, 20
Brown, E. J. (Bomber) Pte 148

Brumfield, I. R. W. (Lou) Lt 92, 160, 169, 184
Buck, D. P. Cpl 96
Buckland, L. E. Cpl 96, 102
Butler, G. A. (Geof) Pte 28

Callander, J. W. (Cal) Capt 20, 22, 93, 117
Cape, G. (George) Pte 28
Carmichael, A. (Hoagie) Cpl 127
Carr, V. N. (Vic) Pte 27, 169, 175
Changhowon-ni 86
Charlesworth, N. R. (Noel, Chic) Lt 23, 28, 29
Chilcott, R. G. (Ray) Pte 28
Chisan attack 133
Chitts, W. J. (Bill) Capt 14, 19, 20, 28
Chongju Battle 14, 15
Church, J. M. (John) Lt 61, 91, 92, 93, 95, 97, 99, 108, 115, 122, 123, 124, 134, 136
Clark, L. G. (Algy) Lt 20, 30, 31, 44
Clark, S. F. (Nobby) Cpl 116, 148, 167, 170, 174
Coad, B. (Basil) Brig 7, 12, 15, 26, 69
Cooper, G. O. Pte 148

INDEX

Crawley, L. W. S/Sgt 31

Denness, A. P. (Arch) Maj 20, 106
"Doctor", Hill 195 113
Donovan, G. D. (Charlie) Cpl 28, 70
Dowsett, A. A. Sgt 117
Duncan, S. J. (Stewart, Stewy) Cpl 94
Dunque, R. E. (Ron) 178

Everleigh, C. J. (Jim, Evileye) Cpl 93, 95, 97, 169

Ferguson, I. B. Lt Col 17, 26, 30, 114, 117, 146, 160, 180, 182
Fielden, D. (Dennis) Lt 164
Fisher, R. Pte 136
Fraser, D. (Uki) Sgt 176

Gallaway, J. F. (Jack) Sgt 21, 65, 101
Gardner, J. F. (Fred) Lt 107, 108, 115, 122, 126, 147, 167
Gay, H. (Hobart) Gen 15
Gerke, J. (Jack) Capt 144
Goldsmith, B. J. (Bernie) Pte 168
Gordon, R. A. (Speed) Maj 10
Gravener, W. N. (Norm) Capt 157, 171, 175, 177, 178, 183
Green, C. H. (Charlie) Lt Col 3, 4, 6, 7, 8, 11, 12, 14, 15, 16, 17, 30, 37, 128
Green, Olwyn Mrs 128
Griffiths, L. C. (Darky) WOII 175
Guest, R. (Robert, Abdul) Pte 144
Gwyther, K. R. Pte 185

Hall, C. C. (Cyril) Capt 24, 76
Hanway, A. P. (Paddy) Maj 139, 140
Harris, G. D. (George) Sgt 32, 35, 45, 55, 72, 92, 123, 134, 136, 147, 148, 161, 175
Harrison, W. J. C. (Bill) WOI 21
Hatfield, K. J. (Kevin) Pte 165
Hayes, T. P. (Tom) Pte 174
Healy, V. T. (Vince) Sgt 125, 128
Hewiston, B. G. (Lofty, Brian) Pte 33, 76, 78, 125, 144, 154
Hollis, T. H. J. (Tom) Pte 96, 101
Honnor, H. B. (Harry) Capt 91
Hummerston, K. J. (Ken) Capt 7
Hunt, E. W. (Buzz) Maj 164, 183

Ichon patrol 94
Indian Fd Amb 150

Jillett, W. E. (Bill, Sailor) Pte 169

Kaesong 8
Kealy, C. (Clem) Cpl 94, 98, 157, 163, 165
Kemp, R. C. Gnr 164
Keys, W. (Bill) Capt 23, 120, 126
K Force 3, 31
Kim, Clang Keun, Mrs 128
King's Own Scottish Borderers 150
King's Shropshire Light Infantry 150
Koch, Kenneth W. Lt 159, 160

INDEX

Koonsey, D. (David) L/Cpl 28
Kunchon 8

Laing, A. W. A. (Padre)
  Chaplain 129, 130, 131
Larkin, J. K. (Keith) Pte 130
Larson, E. O. (Eric) Lt 9, 19
Laughlin, D. P. (Darcy) Capt
  19, 157, 160, 162, 164,
  165, 176, 180
Learmonth, M. E. (Merv) Pte
  125
Lenoy, S. K. (Lennie) Sgt
  158, 162, 168
Light, E. G. Pte 96, 102
Lisk, T. F. (Ted) 122, 135
Luski, C. H. (Colin) Gnr 164

MacArthur, Douglas Gen 22,
  25, 28, 38, 47, 69
Madden, H. W. (Slim) Pte 33
Maher, L. V. (Lofty) Pte 136
Maletz, E. (Lofty) Pte 28, 175
Mann, W. C. (Bill) S/Sgt 31,
  161
Mannett, D. J. (Dave) Lt 14,
  178
Mavin, K. W. (Bluey) Pte 29
McDonald, A. P. (Angus) Lt
  45, 92, 95, 96, 97, 98, 99,
  101, 102, 103
McGavin, P. J. (Sticks) WOII
  20
McGibbon, Ian 164
McGregor, C. C. (Colin) Sgt
  160
McGregor, K. D. (Ken) Lt 176
McHenry, W. R. (Butch) Cpl
  135
McWilliams, R. J. Lt 178
Middlesex Regt 2, 8, 14, 50,
  113, 144, 150, 155, 157

Mitchell, C. (Colin) Capt 134
Monclar Lt Col 108
Montgomerie, L. M. (Monty)
  Lt 176, 177
Moore, Bryant, Maj Gen 108
Morrison, A. L. (Alby) Lt 12
Muggleton, T. L. (Tom) WOII
  35, 55, 72, 115, 118, 144,
  154, 161
Mulligan, R. G. Gnr 164
Mulry, H. (Harold) Lt 32, 33,
  68, 80, 92, 96, 98, 115,
  122, 125, 126, 127, 147,
  148, 169, 174
Muncy, C. R. (Cliff) Pte 31,
  41, 108
Murdoch, R. L. A. (Bob) Capt
  144, 154, 160, 161, 167,
  174, 182, 183, 184, 185

Neilson, Lt Col 9
NZ Field Regt 91, 150, 154,
  155, 157, 160, 177
Nord, C. J. (Cliff) Sgt 136
Nunan, R. (Roy) Pte 34, 59,
  64, 66, 67, 69, 71, 86, 107,
  133, 144

Origlassi, F. J. (Fred) L/Cpl 29
Osbaldiston, M. J. (Ossie) Pte
  91, 125, 168
Outridge, K. P. (Paddy) Capt
  49

Pakchon Battle 18
Parsons, J. D. (Don) Pte 181
Perkins, W. R. (Ron) Sgt 166,
  182, 183, 184
Phillips, E. B. (Fr Joe)
  Chaplain 129, 130, 131
Prior, A. (Arthur) Pte 168
Princess Patricia's Canadian

Light Infantry 118, 120, 150, 155, 184
Pusan 2, 5, 7
Pyongyang 10

RAAF 77 Fighter Sqn 19, 28
RAN 2
Reid, Ian Correspondent 106
Ridgway, Matthew B. Gen 69, 70, 87, 103, 109, 151
Rimmer, A. (Allan) Pte 169
Robertson, Sir Horace Lt Gen 3, 5, 17, 26, 106
Robinson, A. R. Sgt 31, 41, 108
Robinson, F. C. Salvation Army Rep 129, 131
Rowlinson, W. J. (Bill) Cpl 177

Sariwon 9
Saunders, R. (Reg) Capt 32, 43, 44, 58, 59, 66, 76, 78, 91, 118, 123, 133, 134, 144, 157, 181
Scholl, C. (Charlie) Sgt 28, 29, 80, 92, 125, 127, 128
Scott, D. J. (Don) Lt 164, 177
Seoul 1, 5, 7
Servos, M. (Mick) Pte 28, 135
Sheppard, J. T. (Jack) Cpl 92, 115
Sinclair, W. W. (Bill) Cpl 169
Sketchley, K. G. Pte 7
Slim, John Capt 108
Sloane, Maj 9

Smith, D. K. (Smiffy, Dave) Pte 33, 67, 71, 78, 86
Smith, H. L. P. Cpl 127
Stafford, J. Pte 14
Sukchon 10
Svenson, V. K. (Vic) Sgt 30, 32, 35, 44, 92, 167

Taegu 7
Taylor, L. W. (Lennie) Cpl 31, 74
Taylor, T. R. Pte 31, 108
Tokchong withdrawal 75
Townsend, C. (Colin) Lt 13

Vardanegar, Capt 20

Walsh, F. S. (Stan) Lt Col 3, 17, 20, 26
Ward, J. C. (John) Lt 54, 171
Wathem, J. (Joppy) Lt 14
Watson, T. M. (Tommy) Sgt 28
Williams, F. (Fred) Pte 136
Wilson, David, Maj 18
Wilson, R. (Bobby) Pte 28
"Woodbine", Hill 410 attack 120
Woods, W. A. Pte 136

Yongju 10
Yopa-ri 51, 52
Young, J. H. A. (Jim) Capt 184
Yung Kim Choy 62